Week by Week

A Year's Worth of Journaling Prompts
&
Meditations

Amber Lea Starfire

MoonSkye Publishing
Napa, California

Week by Week

Copyright © 2011 by Amber Lea Starfire

All rights reserved.

Cover photography and design © 2011 by Amber Lea Starfire

ISBN: 978-0-9848636-0-0

For Rich

CONTENTS

Table of Contents

Week by Week

INTRODUCTION

Week by Week: A Year's Worth of Journaling Prompts &
Meditations is a collection of journal writing prompts I created
and published in various blogs, newsletters, and articles during
the last two years, from April 2009 through mid-2011.
Although most of these prompts are available online, I felt
inspired to bring them together in a portable collection—
something journal writers could carry with them wherever they
might like to write—the coffeehouse, beach, or park. A
collection that can be used in classrooms and writing groups,
in print and e-book forms.

To the weekly prompts, I've included additional or revised
meditations—thoughts and reflections—for each topic that
will, hopefully, encourage journal writers to think more deeply
about each subject as they engage in the writing process.

It is my hope that *Week by Week* will encourage new writers
to begin a satisfying journaling practice and, at the same time,
inspire experienced journalers to broaden and deepen their
practice—for better understanding of the past, present, and
future.

Journaling Basics

What It Is

Journal writing, put simply, is recording life's events and your responses to them—feelings, reactions, and thoughts. Most often, this is accomplished by writing in notebook. Yet journaling is versatile; there are no wrong ways to keep a journal. You can use pen and paper, or keep your journal on the computer. Your journal may incorporate writing, art, doodling, photography, and audio recordings. The only "rule," if there is such a thing, is that in order to reap the most benefit from journaling, it must be done regularly—daily or several times a week, rarely less than once a week. Journaling is a habitual, open-ended, and rewarding activity that can be as personal and private, or as impersonal and public, as you want it to be.

What You'll Need

All that is required to journal successfully is paper and a pen or pencil. Following is a list of additional possibilities and recommendations from which to choose:

Paper—lined or unlined notebook or bound journal. I recommend that beginning journalers stick with something

2

inexpensive and attractive. You want it to be the kind of journal that feels just special enough to write in, but not so special that you feel intimidated by the clean white pages or expensive paper. It should also be comfortable, easily accessible, and practical.

Pens—If you like to write with a pen, find one that feels good in your hand. One that glides across the page and feels comfortable to hold for extended periods of time. I like to keep my pen with my journal and use it only for journaling.

Lead Pencils—You may choose to write with a pencil. It can be a simple, yellow #2 school pencil, or a mechanical pencil with a comfortable grip. The main thing, as with the pen, is that it be comfortable in your hand for extended periods.

Colored Pencils—I recommend buying a small set of inexpensive colored pencils. You can draw and doodle in your journal, as well as write. Sometimes I like to write with colors that fit or express my mood.

Crayons—Crayons bring out the playfulness in us, allow us to write like children, scrawl across the page, and color and shade our writing. I recommend keeping a small set of crayons on hand for when the urge to play strikes, or when you feel stuck and want to break out of your mental-emotional box.

Glue stick—Keep a glue stick on hand for those times you want to paste a photo, ticket, or some other important memorabilia from your day into your journal. I don't do this often myself, but have found it to be helpful to capture a memory visually, as well as in words.

Computers and Software—I prefer to journal on my computer. However, I recommend that beginning journal writers stick to pen and paper. It's more accessible and, until you've developed a regular journaling habit, the more "organic" and portable tools of pen and paper are a better choice. Once journaling has become a routine part of your life, you might want to try some of the different journaling software programs that are available.

Why Journal?

The number of reasons to journal regularly are as long and varied as one's imagination, and I have a series of articles on my website, WritingThroughLife.com, dedicated to answering the question, "Why Write?" The following list lays out some of the reasons why it's beneficial.

1. Numerous studies have shown that journaling on a regular and consistent basis decreases stress. Journal writing moves stress from your body and mind to the page.

2. It gives you time for yourself, away from the demands of others. If you feel guilty when you take time for self-nurturing, remember that taking care of yourself translates—in addition to improving your own emotional health—to being better able to nurture others.

3. Journal writing allows you to tap into your emotions and open the doors to healing and personal growth. Writing about issues and problems on a regular basis can help you heal past emotional wounds, prevent new wounds from festering and speed healing when they do occur.

4. When your mind seems to be a jumble of thoughts, impressions, and emotions, writing brings clarity to your thinking. It helps you organize your thoughts, brings important feelings and priorities to the fore, and improves your analytical skills.

5. Journal writing is empowering. Through journaling you are able to express what you would not be comfortable saying to others.

6. When exploring issues from the past or dreams for the future, you can allow your imagination to lead the way, thus engaging and enhancing your creativity.

7. Journal writing helps you learn how to communicate better with others. You can use journaling to practice writing letters and/or craft ways of presenting ideas to others. And if you write nonfiction memoir or fiction that others read, you will get feedback from your readers about your ability to communicate that you can then use for further practice.

8. It might seem obvious, but sometimes we need to remind ourselves that writing teaches us the craft of writing. The more you practice, the sharper your skills.

9. Writing regularly, preferably every day, helps you discover your personal writing process—the time of day and kinds of activities that work best for you. You will learn how to be more productive as a writer and, as a big bonus, you will develop a natural and consistent writing voice.

10. Finally, journal writing will help you become a more thoughtful reader. You will naturally approach reading from the point of view of a writer, taking in ideas and learning how to better express yourself from every book, article, and essay you read.

Free Writing

Many prompts instruct you to "free write" about a topic, usually for a minimum of ten minutes. Free writing is, as the term implies, writing without structure or restriction. It means to write whatever comes into your head, even if it is only, "I don't know what to write." There is no wrong way to free write; everything is as it should be. Nothing is too silly, self-absorbed, whiny, or any other adjective your critical mind might find to call it. The only rule is that you continue writing, without stopping, for the entire time.

Keeping your pen moving across the page—or fingers on the keyboard—allows you to ignore your inner critic and get your thoughts, uncensored, on the page.

Word Association Exercises

Another prompt you'll often see is a "word association exercise." Unless otherwise instructed, this means to write the prompted word at the top of a fresh journal page. Underneath that, write the next word that pops into your mind. Without stopping, continue to write words on the page until your mind is quiet. It's important not to censor—every word is as valid as any other word. When you're done listing words, the weekly prompt will tell you what to do next.

Now that you understand what journaling is and why to do it, get ready. It's time to begin writing.

HOW TO USE THIS BOOK

I must learn to love the fool in me, the one who feels too much, talks too much, takes too many chances, wins sometimes and loses often, lacks self-control, loves and hates, hurts and gets hurt, promises and breaks promises, laughs and cries.

~ Theodore Isaac Rubin

Though you can respond to the journal writing prompts in the order presented, *Week by Week* has been organized to help you find prompts that are relevant to your life events and interests. Each of the eight general categories—Self-awareness, Authenticity, Family & Relationships, Obstacles & Opportunities, Seasons & Holidays, The World, Spirituality, and Moving Forward—are described in detail below, along with their related topics.

Each topic presents a week's worth of journaling prompts, which encourage you to get beneath surface answers, raise self-awareness, and develop new ways to view the issues you're exploring. The prompts also invite you to engage in a variety of exercises to bring your senses and intuition into the writing process.

One approach to selecting a topic is to slowly scan the chapter titles in the Table of Contents. As you do so, notice which topics give rise to an emotional response—excitement, anger, sadness, or even resistance. Emotional responses often indicate unresolved issues or areas that you subconsciously want to address; the more intense the emotional response, the more important the issue.

You may also choose to select a topic at random, or by relevance to a particular life event, holiday, or season.

Remember that there are no right or wrong ways to select a writing topic, and there are no right or wrong answers to any of the writing prompts. They are offered simply as ways to help you examine and become more aware of the feelings and core beliefs that you hold. Self-knowledge lights the path of personal growth. It empowers you to choose who you want to be and how you present yourself in the world.

Self-Awareness

Meditations and prompts in the "Self-Awareness" category encourage you to examine your assumptions, belief systems, and emotions in order to expand self-knowledge and awareness. Topics include how you present yourself to others through the stories you tell, how you learn, understanding how and why you choose perspectives through which to comprehend life, and your underlying attitudes around giving and receiving, personal freedom, and fear of failure. You'll identify your natural rhythms, consider how to work with them instead of against them, and learn methods to acknowledge and expand your creative expression.

Authenticity

Recognizing your underlying assumptions and belief systems helps you make choices that support living life authentically, on your terms. "Authenticity" moves the journaling discussion one step deeper. You'll define what authenticity means to you, examine its relationship to meaningful action, explore ways to discover and live a passionate life, and look at what it means to live life fully and/or have a fulfilled life (one is something you do, the other is something you have). You will write about speaking your truths to yourself and others, and explore what joy and happiness each mean to you, as well as how to experience these positive emotions more often.

Family & Relationships

In this section, you have the opportunity to explore and write about different aspects of relationship—from family and friendship, to how you build community. You'll take a close look at what friendship means to you and the ways in which you do and do not include friends in your life. You'll explore your deeper truths about family relationships, crises, and emotional vulnerability, as well as attitudes and beliefs about money and how they affect your close relationships. Finally, you'll examine the importance of personal community and how you build a support community as a journaler and writer.

Obstacles & Opportunities

The prompts in this broadly categorized section will help you explore how you deal with externally and internally imposed limitations, how you do or do not set boundaries, and how important control is to your sense of safety and security. Topics include the line between desire and reality, ways in which you overcome obstacles, setting boundaries through saying "yes" and "no," and different ways to perceive time. "Obstacles and Opportunities" topics will help you gain a greater understanding of the effects of physical limitations and how you deal with them, as well as explore the ways you deal with feelings of stress, resistance, helplessness, and lack of control.

Seasons & Holidays

In "Seasons & Holidays," you'll look at the effects and meanings of seasons and seasonal holidays with prompts on endings and beginnings, passing of the seasons, memories from your youth, emotional associations with various holidays during the year, and how death and loss play into your responses to each season.

The World

"The World" writing prompts encourage you to reflect on the larger world outside your personal life events and experiences, as well as explore your political and social beliefs and attitudes. These prompts cover politics, your views on human nature, war and peace, consumerism, the economy, technology and the Internet. Topics also include how and why to record current events in your journal, and what it means to be interdependent with others.

Spirituality

The topics in this section help you take a deeper look at your personal motivations, reasons and expressions of gratitude, the kinds of metaphor you use to frame your views of life, ways to get beneath the surface of easy answers, what it means to be present, and ways to see the extraordinary in the everyday ordinary.

Moving Forward

"Moving Forward" will help you discover ways to expand your journal writing practice and generate your own writing prompts.

Week by Week

SELF-AWARENESS

WHAT'S YOUR STORY?

The past is not simply the past, but a prism through which the subject filters his own changing self-image.

~ Doris Kearns Goodwin

It happens all the time. Someone says, "Tell me a little about yourself," asks, "What do you do?" or I have to introduce myself to a group, so I grab a piece of my history, mix it with a bit of now, and spin a tale for my audience. The protagonist is always me and, depending on time, may be the only character in my story.

How do we choose what to tell someone or a group when our time is limited? Perhaps the larger question is, how do we choose to define ourselves to others? Does this telling reflect what we see in the mirror, or is it a piece of fiction designed to make a good impression? What are the differences between our private and public stories, and our reasons for telling them?

This Week's Writing Prompts

1. When someone asks, "What do you do?" what do you say? And do you begin with, "I am ..." or "I work ..." or some

other verb? In what ways do you identify yourself with the work or the things you do on a daily basis? And, in what ways do you separate who you are from what you do?

2. How is what you say to a professional group or individual different than what you say to an informal group (such as a club) or individual? Write about the differences in the ways you present yourself and the reasons for the differences. Do you try to make yourself sound "better" than you believe yourself to be when introducing yourself in the professional realm? Why or why not?

3. What would you prefer that no one know about you, and why?

4. What would you like everyone to know about you, and why?

5. If you could be truly vulnerable, let down your guard, and tell your true story to someone you've just met, without fear of judgment, what would you say?

6. How do you define your life? Do you consider your true story to be primarily one of pain or happiness? Do you think of your life as mostly easy or mostly difficult? Is it possible to see the events in your life from another perspective? For example, if you've viewed your life as mostly difficult and/or painful, how would your life be perceived from the point of view of someone in extreme poverty, or from a continually war-torn country? And if you think of your life as mostly easy, what kind of person might consider your life difficult? How does viewing your life from these other perspectives inform your story telling?

7. Complete the following sentences:

I am ...

I love ...

I grew up ...

I live ...

I want to ...

Free write for ten minutes about the answers you gave and how they contribute to your life story.

THE ROAD TO LEARNING

We write before knowing what to say and how to say it, and in order to find out, if possible."

~ Jean-Francois Lyotard

I forget what keyed the idea, but I started thinking about the act of learning and how different it is for each of us. By learning, I mean the process through which we acquire skills and knowledge—learning because something interests us, because acquiring those skills or that knowledge moves us farther down the path of life we want to walk, not because the subject is forced upon us as in high school, and some workplaces.

As human beings, we are constantly learning and growing. It's part of who we are by definition. Over the years, there's been a lot of talk about learning styles. Right vs. left-brain learning, holistic vs. serial, dependent vs. independent, reflective vs. impulsive, visual vs. auditory or kinesthetic. And, of course, none of us learn in only one of these ways, but in unique combination of them.

What do you do when you want to learn something new? Some people enjoy structure and go about learning in a linear fashion. For example, when I was eight years old, my mother gave me an old Royal typewriter and a dog-eared college typing text that she'd picked up at a garage sale. I fantasized about being a writer and, on my own, worked my way lesson by lesson through that text. When I was done, I typed an accurate 35 or 40 words per minute. (Pretty good for an eight-year-old, huh?)

When I want to know how to do something, I investigate my topic, decide on a path of action, and then move through it step by step. For knowledge-based learning, I do well in traditional schools. If it's something that requires practice, I'll set up a schedule and pretty much stick to it. I thrive on goals and schedules and learn well on my own, but always appreciate a mentor or teacher—someone who can guide and push me to excel.

Others approach it in a roundabout fashion, circling their subject as though it is prey and they are its predators. They pick aspects of the skill and learn those as they have time. They might be socially oriented and surround themselves with people who are involved in their chosen skill—clubs, social groups, etc.

Learning is an active process. You need to practice to learn a physical skill, such as typing or dancing or driving. Even learning a piece of knowledge requires some practice in reading, repetition, and memory. Still, we each have our own unique ways of acquiring skills that are important to us.

What are your ways, and how do yours fit into standard learning models?

This Week's Writing Prompts

1. Define what learning something new means to you.

2. Write about your relationship to the process of learning. Do you enjoy it? Look forward to it? Dread it? Feel that it's necessary or unnecessary?

3. Write about your first experience with school, perhaps when you entered kindergarten or first grade. What were your expectations, and what happened?

4. Write about your high school experience. How did you feel about attending high school? Were you still learning? Was it mostly a social experience? What would you have done if you could have changed your experience in any way?

5. If you went to college, write about what you hoped to learn at that time. Did you change your major? Did you learn what you wanted to learn? Was it a meaningful experience? If you didn't go to college, write about the factors that influenced your decision not to go and what that means to you now.

6. Write your response to the following quote by Lloyd Alexander: *We learn more by looking for the answer to a question and not finding it than we do from learning the answer itself.* Do you think this is true? Why or why not?

7. If you could learn anything new right now, what would it be? Is there anything holding you back? What is it, and what would you need to do to start learning about this topic or skill?

WHAT'S YOUR PERSPECTIVE?

A purely objective viewpoint does not exist in the cosmos or in politics.

~ Howard Fineman

I've been thinking a lot about who I am when I write—and I don't mean who I identify myself to be in this life, but who I am as a narrator—because when I journal, I can write from so many different perspectives.

Depending on what I'm writing about, I can be the wounded victim, the wise grandmother, the young child, all three, or someone entirely different. Which perspective serves me best depends on the story I want to tell and whether it's for myself, in my journal, or for others, as in memoir or personal essay. Each of these perspectives is real and true to me as a person, but the way that a story is communicated and perceived is a function of who the narrator is.

This week's journaling prompts are designed to help you be more aware of who you are as the narrator of your own life story.

This Week's Writing Prompts

1. Read a random sampling of seven past journal entries.
    Identify and label who was narrating each journal entry.
    What role were you playing? What perspective did you
    give?

2. Think of a time in your life when you felt hurt by someone
    else's actions. Write about that event from the viewpoint
    of the victim. Now, write about the same event from the
    other person's viewpoint, in effect playing devil's advocate
    with your victim narrator. Read the two different versions.
    What can you learn from writing about something from
    these two different viewpoints?

3. Pick a third viewpoint—casual observer, wise older person,
    mature adult, or some other person, and write another
    version of the story, combining the three viewpoints.

4. Write about a problem you had today, then write about it
    as though you are writing from a distance of five years in
    the future. What is the difference in tone? Does the
    problem seem as important to your future self as your
    today self?

5. Another way to think about perspective, is to think about
    it in terms of distance. In prompt number 4, you wrote
    from a different time perspective. Pick an event in your life
    and write about it from two different physical perspectives.
    For example, if today I had a conversation with my
    daughter, I could write about the conversation in first
    person present tense, as a participant, or I could write
    about it in third person past tense, as though I were
    someone looking in the window, reporting what I had seen
    and heard. How might your story be different when told
    from a different physical perspective?

7. Pick an object. Describe it when viewed up close—*extremely* up close—and when seen from across the room. What do you notice about the object in each case that you didn't notice in the other?

8. Select a current emotional issue in your life, either negative or positive. Write about that issue from a negative point of view (cynical, pessimistic, angry, whatever). Now write about the same issue from a positive point of view (trusting, optimistic, joyful).

Do you usually write from the same perspective? If so, what is it? What can you learn about yourself through writing from different viewpoints?

GIVING AND RECEIVING

You cannot hold on to anything good. You must be continually giving—and getting. You cannot hold on to your seed. You must sow it—and reap anew. You cannot hold on to riches. You must use them and get other riches in return.

~ Robert Collier

When we think about gift giving and receiving, we usually think about the tangible kind. But giving isn't always about tinsel and glitter and money. There are so many ways to give to others. Smiles, hugs, kind words, compliments, picking up after others, offering patience, acts of kindness, and forgiveness are all gifts that cost nothing but time and intention.

The other side of giving—receiving—is just as important. In particular, receiving love and help from others can be difficult. But in many ways, receiving with gratitude is as much giving as it is receiving. Think about a time you wanted to do something nice for someone, only to have your offer rejected. If the person had received your gift with an open heart, wouldn't that have been a wonderful gift to you?

Writing Prompts about Giving

1. When you think of gifts, do you generally think of the kind you buy, the kind you make, or the kind you do? Write about the different kinds of giving, which gives you the most satisfaction, and why.

2. Do you give on a regular basis to individuals and/or charities? Who do you usually give to, and why? What about those individuals or organizations inspires your generosity?

3. Do you enjoy giving gifts on traditional gift giving days, such as birthdays, Valentine's Day, Mother's Day, and Christmas, or do you think of them as obligations to be met? Write about particular gift giving traditions that you find difficult, as well as those that you look forward to.

4. Free write for at least ten minutes about the word *generosity*. What do you think about/associate with it? Do you know any generous people? What makes them generous? Do you consider yourself to be generous? Why or why not? And so on ...

Writing Prompts about Receiving

1. Have you ever wanted to give something to someone and had him or her reject your gift? How did you feel? Were you disappointed? Did you take it in stride? Write about how it feels when a gift you want to give is rejected.

2. How do you feel about receiving help when you need it, or unsolicited compliments? Do you find receiving in these cases difficult to do? What feelings does receiving bring up, and do you experience these feelings as negative or positive?

3. Write about how you typically respond when someone offers help that you know you need, and how you respond

when someone offers you a compliment. What do you notice about these two ways of receiving?

4. Look around your home. Choose one item and make a list of all the people who helped bring it to you: farmers, harvesters, factory workers, truckers, pilots, mail persons, packaging facilities, retail clerks, etc. Make the list as complete as possible. What do you think about the idea of receiving this item through the efforts of so many people?

IF THEY REALLY KNEW YOU

Truth never lost ground by enquiry.

~ Lord Byron

In July of 2010, MTV began airing a series titled "If You Really Knew Me," named after a conversation prompt coined by Rich and Yvonne Dutra-St. John, Founders of the nonprofit organization, Challenge Day. The organization leads experiential workshops for teens and their parents designed to help the participants understand that, no matter what they're going through, they are not alone, and that it is possible to live in a world where love, connection, truth, and full expression are the norm instead of the exception. The series followed Challenge Day facilitators as they led these workshops in various high schools around the United States.

Having once worked for the organization and attended a number of these workshops, I can attest that they actually work to break down artificial barriers between people and get to the heart of what we have in common—our joy and our pain—in short, our humanity.

Browsing news feeds on the Internet recently, I encountered global reports of murder, poor economies, politicians fighting with one another, and people disconnecting from one another. Where is the good news? I thought. Then I remembered Challenge Day, and their vision for all children to "live in a world where they feel safe, loved, and celebrated."

So many of us are steeped in the idea that reality is necessarily negative. (My mother once told me that reality meant "death, war, and taxes.") But is that truly true? Do we have to relegate all the good stuff to "fantasy" and all the bad stuff to "reality"? Or is this something we've come to believe because that's what we've been taught?

This week's writing prompts help us to explore our personal sense of reality, what it means to be vulnerable, and what we hope for the future.

This Week's Writing Prompts

1. Do you think that violence and war are an inevitable truth about humankind? What in your own life experience confirms your viewpoint? Now, dig a little deeper and write about what you've seen or experienced that contradicts your viewpoint.

2. Write about emotional vulnerability. What happens when we open up to others and share our thoughts and fears and dreams? Do we get closer to or further away from them?

3. When you think about the topic of separation and loneliness in the world, how do you feel? Do you avoid the topic? What is your emotional reaction and what do you do about it?

4. What is the difference between peace and compassion?

5. Do you believe that it's possible to live in a society, or a subset of society, where children feel safe, loved and celebrated? What do you think it would take to create such a society?

6. Write a response to the following: *It is lack of love for ourselves that inhibits our compassion toward others. If we make friends with ourselves, then there is no obstacle to opening our hearts and minds to others.*

7. Free write for at least ten minutes, starting with completing the following sentence: *If you really knew me, you'd know ...*

ON FREEDOM

Conformity is the jailer of freedom and the enemy of growth.
~ John F. Kennedy

I've been thinking about freedom—what it has meant to me in the past and what it means to me now; how my desire for freedom has, in many ways, shaped my desires and many of my decisions; and how it may influence my future.

Before we get into this week's journaling prompts, let's take a look at the dictionary definition of freedom as excerpted from dictionary.com (I've included only those definitions that refer to personal freedom):

- the state of being at liberty rather than in confinement or under physical restraint;
- exemption from external control, interference, regulation, etc.;
- exemption from the presence of anything specified (usually followed by from): freedom from fear;
- the absence of or release from ties, obligations, etc.;
- ease or facility of movement or action;

- the right to enjoy all the privileges or special rights of citizenship, membership, etc., in a community or the like;
- the right to frequent, enjoy, or use at will;
- the power to exercise choice and make decisions without constraint from within or without; autonomy; self-determination.

As you can see, personal freedom is a many-faceted concept, which we can explore from different points of view.

This week's prompts are designed to help you delve more deeply into your understanding of personal freedom and its influence in your life.

This week's writing prompts

1. Write about a past moment in your life when you felt most free. What was it about that event, time, or activity that gave you such a sense of freedom? What were its qualities? What were you free from, and what were you free to do?

2. Thinking about that past moment of freedom, how do you experience (or not experience) that same kind of freedom in your life now?

3. On a scale of 1 to 10, where 1 is completely constrained and 10 is completely free, where do you place yourself today? Write about the reasons you placed yourself on that point in the scale.

4. List the qualities of freedom you wrote about in prompt number 1. Feel free to add to that list. Then, prioritize them. Which qualities are most important to you? For example, if my list includes autonomy (not having to answer to anyone else), freedom of movement, and

freedom from worry, I might place autonomy first, freedom of movement second, and freedom from worry third.

5. Have you ever had a time in your life when you felt constrained, trapped, or imprisoned in some way? Free write about that time and how it affected (and continues to affect) your subsequent life decisions.

6. Do you believe that freedom is given to you by others, or created by you? Explain.

7. Finally, how important is freedom to you today? What do you give up for personal freedom, if anything (e.g., security, safety, relationships)? Finally, what and who do you think have most influenced your attitudes and beliefs regarding personal freedom?

RESPECTING OUR NATURAL RHYTHMS

Everything has rhythm. Everything dances.
~ Maya Angelou

Every living thing—animals, plants and even bacteria—has a circadian rhythm. The word *circadian*, originating in Latin, means *around the day*, or *approximately one day*. Daily rhythms are adjusted by environmental factors, such as daylight, but we each have a unique built-in clock that governs our most and least energetic times of day and affects the way we think, feel, and act.

Although there is a more-or-less typical circadian rhythm for humans—we are most alert at 10:00 a.m., most physically coordinated at 2:30 p.m., have the highest body temperature at 7:00 p.m., and sleep most deeply at 2:00 a.m.— there is a great deal of variation among us. And we have titles for the divergent: *night owls*, for those more productive in the late hours of the evening, and *morning birds*, for those who rise full of energy while the sun is still yawning. Even within our individual rhythms, these internal clocks shift over time, affected by hormonal changes, such as adolescence, pregnancy, menopause, and advanced age. (Teenagers sometimes seem more related to vampires than humans in terms of their sleeping habits.)

Recently I have once again become acutely aware of how important it is to honor our circadian rhythms. When we don't, we end up paying the price: we feel peevish and out of sorts, our blood sugar drops, and we can't think. We yell at our loved ones, make mistakes at work and at home—potentially catastrophic ones. All this because we didn't listen to the basic needs of our bodies.

My last two weeks were great examples. Between semesters of graduate school, I thought it would be a great idea to cram all my long-awaited family visits together. In doing so, I put myself in situations where my own rhythms and energy cycles were ignored, resulting in the kind of exhaustion that makes me wonder what on earth I was thinking when I contrived that schedule.

Even when we don't create these situations for ourselves, we sometimes find ourselves in circumstances where it seems impossible to honor our natural cycles: we have newborns, aging parents, or others we need to care for; we have jobs with the wrong hours; we have responsibilities and commitments.

We can't control our circadian rhythms and we can't always control life's circumstances, but we can spend some time thinking and writing about the subject, come to know ourselves more deeply, and be more conscious about our needs as we make decisions for the future.

This Week's Writing Prompts

1. Describe your natural daily rhythm. If you didn't set an alarm, what time of day would you awake? When are you usually most/least productive? Do you prefer to go to bed early or late? When are you naturally hungry?

2. Do your natural rhythms fit the life you lead? If so, did you consciously arrange your life to fit your needs or did it just "seem to happen"? If not, what factors have made it difficult to meet the needs of your circadian rhythm?

3. If you could arrange your life around your natural rhythms, what would your day look like? Allow your imagination to run free and write everything down, whether or not you think your description realistic.

4. Thinking about your circadian rhythm, complete the following sentence: *All my life* ... Write for at least ten minutes.

5. David Blask, Ph.D., M.D., a researcher on circadian rhythm disruption said, "Evidence is emerging that disruption of one's circadian clock is associated with cancer in humans, and that interference with internal timekeeping can tip the balance in favor of tumor development." How do you feel about this statement?

6. Thinking about how your natural rhythms do or do not conform to society's expectations, complete the following sentences: *I feel frustrated that* ... and *I feel satisfied that* ... Write for at least ten minutes.

7. How does your rhythm fit, or not fit, with the rhythms of your family and loved ones? Do differences in circadian rhythm cause conflicts? How can understanding your own and others' natural rhythms increase your capacity for compassion and tolerance?

Fear of Failure

Failure too is a form of death.

~ Graham Greene

We all share a particular kind of fear—the kind that can stop us before we begin learning a new skill or start a new venture, the kind that seethes beneath the surface of every creative act, the kind that began in us when we were young children.

This fear sometimes causes us to be reluctant to take risks unless success, however we measure it, is assured. We might think of it as a fear of making mistakes, of not achieving, or of simply making a "fool" of ourselves in some way. If we give in to it, this fear can hold us back from doing the very things we long to do: write, paint, get that new job, or meet that special person.

It is the fear of failure.

This week's writing prompts

1. Define what it means for you to succeed at something. Where do you think you got these ideas about success?

2. When was the first time you remember experiencing failure? What happened? Who was involved and why did it feel like failure? Did someone tell you that you failed? Were you derided or made fun of in any way? Did you try again, or did you give up, and how did you feel later?

3. Do a word association exercise with the word *failure*. Look over the resulting list. What do you notice? How do you feel as you read? Now perform the same exercise with the word *success*. Again, what do you notice and how do you feel as you read the words? Free write for ten minutes about this exercise.

4. Describe a time when you were so afraid of failure that you decided not to attempt something new. Then describe a time when you were afraid of failure, but you attempted whatever it was you had in mind anyway. What were the results each time, and why, the second time, did you decide to go ahead with the effort? What was at stake?

5. If a person continues trying to achieve something, even after they have not achieved it the first, second, or even third time around, is their lack of achievement failure? Why or why not?

6. Is failure a subjective or objective term? Explain.

7. Do you know anyone who has let a fear of failure hold him or her back? If so, describe this person in detail—talents, gifts, personality, and what you perceive as his potential. If you don't know anyone like that, describe what you imagine that person would be like.

EXPANDING YOUR CREATIVITY

A hunch is creativity trying to tell you something.

~ Frank Capra

Everyone is born creative—it's human nature. But as we grow and become socialized, we learn that "creative" is generally a word used to describe artists and musicians and craftspeople. People with "talent." Probably not us.

At some point during our lives, though, we realize that creativity is a much broader concept: it's about doing something in a new way, producing something novel or different, or finding an elegant solution to a complicated problem.

If you've experienced this realization, perhaps you've begun to suspect you're creative after all. Perhaps you've begun to express yourself in traditionally creative ways, such as writing and art, but maybe you've chosen to express your creativity in other ways, through problem solving at work, for example.

Expressing creativity is fun, but it's also hard work, like a muscle that must be conditioned in order for healthy functioning and growth.

This week's prompts and activities are designed to help you tap into and exercise your natural creativity.

This week's writing prompts

1. Remember a happy moment in your life. Allow yourself to be bathed in that memory, so that it makes you smile and you feel the glow of those happy emotions. Remember another happy moment. And another. Then complete the following sentence: *I am most happy when ...*

2. Do a word association with the word *creativity*. Using your list of words, create a word and image collage. Write the words on separate pieces of paper, or cut them from magazines, and pair them with images. Paste these words and images in whatever arrangement feels good to you on a page of your journal, or something larger if you prefer.

3. Get angry! That's right, let that righteous indignation about the political or economic situation take over. Release your anger over being mistreated by someone, or the mistreatment of someone else. Get furious, and write your fury onto the page.

4. Make spontaneous sounds. Make noise with your body. Claps, slaps, hoots, and hollers. Anything but words. Do this for at least two minutes (use a timer). You may feel silly, but do it anyway. Then, sit down and free write about the experience.

5. Make a list of all your positive attributes. Are you a gifted cook? Musician? Accountant? Are you healthy and fit? When you are done, at the top of the page write "gifts." Write about how you might use each of these gifts in a way new to you.

6. Take a nap. Okay. This one's not really a journaling prompt. But I guarantee that nap taking enhances creativity!

7. Take time by yourself for yourself: make a date to nurture yourself this week. It can be as simple as taking the time to go to the park, appreciate a full moon, get a massage, or take yourself out to dinner. The "what" is up to you. After you've gone on that date, write in your journal about your time with yourself. What did you think about? What was your emotional state before and afterwards?

AUTHENTICITY

AUTHENTICITY AND MEANING

The significance of a man is not in what he attains, but rather what he longs to attain.

~ Khalil Gibran

As a part-time photographer, I have photographed a number of high school graduation ceremonies. Pomp and Circumstance, school bands, the Pledge of Allegiance, and speeches by school administrators and student valedictorians are all part of the graduation rites to which we have become accustomed. I always wonder why people feel the need for so many speeches. All the young graduates want is to walk across that stage, receive their diplomas, throw their hats in the air, and begin a well-deserved celebration before moving on to the next phase of their lives.

By far, the best and—in my mind—most authentic speech I heard during these ceremonies was given by an earnest graduate who said that her goal, when writing her speech, was not to give another trite graduation speech, the "this is the first day of the rest of your lives" kind of speech, but to say something meaningful. She said that every day is a new beginning and that we should be asking ourselves, each day,

42

how we are making meaning of our lives. Heady and mature words for such a young woman.

She went on to tell the story of how, during her freshman year, she became involved in the Amnesty International club and engaged in activities related to human rights and social justice. She talked about how she wrote letters and made phone calls while, all along, wondering if her efforts were making any difference. Finally, she decided that even if her efforts were not changing the world, they had changed *her*. She was making a conscious effort to make this world a better place and it had the effect of giving her life more meaning. She urged all of her fellow graduates to make a commitment to doing something for someone else at least once each day and to consciously engage in acts that would give their lives more meaning.

Needless to say, I was impressed by her maturity and presence of mind. I was also moved by her words, which made me think about how sheltered and insulated from the world I tend to become, sometimes more like an ostrich with her head in the sand than the bold and intrepid writer I would like to believe I am. Her words made me think about the ways I make meaning in my own life.

Merriam Webster defines the word *meaning* as: "something meant or intended, a significant quality; especially implication of a hidden or special significance."

I believe that all of our lives are authentic and meaningful in some way, even when we're unconscious of the fact. The trick is to become conscious and aware of the impact and meaning of our actions while they are yet in motion.

This Week's Writing Prompts

1. What is your initial reaction to the story of the young graduation speaker? What is your emotional response to the idea that what we do changes us?

2. In what ways do you feel that your life is and is not full of meaning?

3. Do you engage in regular activities that feel meaningful to you? If so, what are those activities, and what satisfaction do they give you? Would you do them more if you could?

4. Can you think of something that seems satisfying to you that would not be satisfying or meaningful for someone else you know, and vice versa? How do you feel when others disregard something you care deeply about? Do others' feelings and opinions affect whether or not you act on what you care about?

5. What is your emotional reaction to the following words by John F Kennedy? *One person can make a difference and every person should try.*

6. Do a ten-minute, free association on the word *authenticity*.

7. If you could do one thing that would make a small, but real, difference for someone you love, what would it be? If you could make a small, but real, difference to your community, what would it be? And finally, if you could make a small, but real, difference to the world, what would it be? For one or more of these situations, describe what you would do, what the difference would be, and how you would feel by accomplishing this change.

FINDING YOUR PASSION

Chase down your passion like it's the last bus of the night.

~ Terri Guillemets

However you want to describe it, when you follow your heart, do what you love, or live your passion, you are doing the things that are so exceedingly fun, so joyful, that you lose track of time. Each day, you are excited about your work. You may even feel guilty, as though feeling alive and happy is unlawful.

But what if you don't know what you love? Or love so many things that you get confused and can't focus on just one? The following prompts will help you center in on what's most important to the passionate, creative part of your being.

This Week's Writing Prompts

1. Make a list of everything you're good at. What are the things that other people ask you to help them with? Think about jobs you've held and things you've accomplished in the past. Next, group your abilities into broad categories, such as organizing, coordinating, building, writing, speaking, and visual art. Do your abilities tend to be visual, verbal, and/or kinesthetic?

2. Now make another list of the kinds of things you like to play at. Think about when you were a child—what kinds of things did you love most to do? As an adult, what hobbies do you enjoy? What kinds of activities do you gravitate towards in your spare time? List everything and then, as in prompt number 1, try to find common elements among the activities. Do they primarily involve movement, art, or communication? Do you prefer activities that are solitary or social?

3. What have you dreamed of doing, either in the past or now? What was/is it about that dream that excites you? What has held you back from pursuing that dream?

4. Next, go down your lists and—as quickly as possible and without thinking about it—assign a value of 1 to 10 to each item, where 1 = least excited and 10 = ecstatic. Do it quickly! It's okay if you end up with a lot of 5's or 10's. Just keep rating. When you're done, pick three items from your list of 10's, based on your emotional attraction to that item when you look at it. For each of the three things, free write for ten minutes about what your life would be like if you could do that for a living. Write about everything: lifestyle, emotions, what your day might look like, and what would change.

5. For each of the three things you chose, write about what you would have to learn and/or research to begin. Who would you need/want to interview? What books would you need to read? What classes would you want to take? How much time would you need to commit to the learning process? Write down all the reasons you can and should make this time commitment.

6. Free write for ten minutes about the fears you have about doing what you think you'd love to do. What might happen? Is it okay to be happy? Why or why not? Write

about the worst and the best that could happen if you decided to do any of the three things that excited you.

7. Write down one step you will take to get started exploring one of those three items you selected. Write down when you will do it. Then write about how you feel knowing that you will be taking positive steps toward exploring your options.

LIVING LIFE FULLY

And in the end, it's not the years in your life that count. It's the life in your years.

~ Abraham Lincoln

On this gray November morning, as I sit in my office in front of the blue-white reflection of my computer screen, I am contemplating what it means to live life 100%, to live all out, to live life fully. Each of us has a different definition of what living fully means, and those definitions are not static; they change, depending upon stage of life, current experiences, and our core energy levels.

When I researched the subject, I discovered that to some, living life fully means dedicating yourself to personal/spiritual development. To others, it means setting and achieving challenging goals, or taking risks. Another approach to living fully is to learn to be present in each moment and, by so doing, experiencing the completeness, and complexity, of each moment. Others believe that living is all about learning to love yourself and others, and that if you learn how to love and be compassionate, you will be more alive. Then there's the hedonistic approach: experience as much as possible in the shortest time possible.

Are any of these approaches the "correct" one? Does it matter? Is living life fully about peace and spirit, or is it about wild experience and exuberant joy? Might it be about all of the above? What do you believe?

This Week's Writing Prompts

1. What does it mean to you, at this time in your life, to "live life fully"?

2. How has this phrase changed for you over the years (when you were 15, 20, 30, and so on)?

3. If you were to discover today that you had a life-threatening disease, would your definition change? If so, how might it change? If not, why do you think it would remain the same?

4. In the second paragraph above, I listed some of the different approaches people take to living their lives fully. Do you think any one of these approaches is better than the other? Why or why not?

5. Are you living fully? If not, do you believe that you can live life fully right now? What is holding you back?

6. Is living life fully all about the big things or the little things? Interpret "big" and "little" however you want. Describe some of these big and little things.

7. Respond to the following quote by Angela Monet: *Those who danced were thought to be quite insane by those who could not hear the music.* What do you think she meant by that? How is this true or not true in your life?

A Fulfilled Life

People want riches; they need fulfillment.

~ Robert Conklin

Each person defines what it means to have a "fulfilled life" in his or her own way. For some, it means following artistic passions, finding the right career, or helping others. For others, it means building satisfying relationships and strong community ties. For still others, it means living a life of adventure and adrenalin-producing risk. But for most of us, it's an individualized balance of all of the above.

I believe that each of us can have a fulfilled life, but that it's also not a static thing. We are always developing, growing, changing, and evolving. Our ideas about what fulfills us changes over time, so that although we may feel perfectly fulfilled at some point, a day or a week later we may feel some vague sense of dissatisfaction and a desire to do something new.

It's fun and enlightening to journal on a regular basis about what makes for a fulfilled life. Over the years, you'll see shifts and spirals and patterns to your desires.

This week's writing prompts

1. Make a list of your criteria for a fulfilled life. Areas to consider: health/fitness, creativity, play, education, financial status, relationships, spirituality, relaxation.

2. Elaborate about each item on your list. For example, if it's important to you to be continually learning new things, what does that look like? How do you imagine making that happen? And why is it important to you?

3. Reflecting on your list, which of those items seems most difficult or least fulfilled for you at this time? Free write for five minutes about perceived obstacles, then free write for five minutes about how you will feel when you have those things in your life. Do you feel that you need to make some changes to feel more fulfilled? What would have to happen? What would you have to say "no" to, and what would you need to say "yes" to?

4. Which of the items on your list do you currently have in your life? Is there anything these have in common? If so, what? And what is most fulfilling about them? For example, perhaps you feel fulfilled in your nursing career and as a mother because you enjoy helping others. Or you feel fulfilled in your artistic career and as a business consultant because you enjoy finding creative solutions to things.

5. Prioritize your list. Recognizing that all of these items are important to you (or you would not have listed them), which one is most important to you and why? Which is least important to you and why?

6. How does your life reflect your current priorities? How does it not?

7. Imagine having everything on your list. Start a new page in your journal, and title it "A Week in the Life of (your name)." Describe a wonderfully fulfilled week. What happens? Who with? What do you do or not do? Have fun with this—there are no limitations.

HONESTY

We wear a mask that grins and lies
It hides our cheeks and shades our eyes
This debt we pay to human guile
With torn and bleeding hearts we smile.
~ Paul Lawrence Dunbar

Writers on journal writing, such as myself, teach that honesty is an important component of journaling—if we want self-knowledge, inspiration, creativity, insight, comfort, and healing. Honesty seems like such an easy thing: "Just be honest with yourself." But what exactly does that mean? Do we *really* want to know why we yell at our kids, can't stop smoking, or stay up too late at night? And even if we want to be honest, how do we tell ourselves the hard truths we don't want to hear?

To be honest means to be free of deceit and untruthfulness. Being free of deceit is more specific than "tell the truth." To be honest with yourself and in your writing requires that you search yourself for pockets and corners of deceit. What truths are you hiding from yourself because they might hurt your feelings?

To be honest also means to be simple and unpretentious. I like this definition, because it speaks of an attitude, not just a standard. When I write simply and unpretentiously, I am much more likely to be free of deceit—to be honest—because pretension is all about trying to be someone other than who I am. I judge myself as not good enough, thus requiring a false persona or mask. The height of self-deceit would be to believe I am that made-up person. But when I have the attitude, "What you see is what you get," then I can also look into the mirror of my writing and reflect upon the person I see in it.

There are different kinds of honesty. For example, emotional honesty, that is, being aware of and expressing our true feelings; intellectual honesty, saying what we truly think; and moral honesty, adhering to facts as much as possible, avoiding deceit.

But, many of us have been raised to hide our emotions, to be polite rather than say what we think, and to deceive through omission while "technically" telling the facts. The habits of deception can be so ingrained, or we may have become so used to distrusting ourselves, that we might not know how we really feel, what we really think, or what the facts really are.

Use the following prompts to become more aware and honest with yourself—emotionally, intellectually, and morally—so you can benefit the most from your writing.

This Week's Writing Prompts

1. When you're so angry with someone that you feel like you hate him or her (even yourself), are you able to write about your anger and hatred honestly? Or do you judge yourself for feeling that way and, instead, write about all the reasons you shouldn't be angry? What do you think would happen if you wrote your hatred honestly on the page?

2. Write about how, as a child, your feelings and thoughts were validated or invalidated. Do you continue those patterns with yourself and with others? Write about ways you can use your writing to validate your feelings and thoughts.

3. What or who are you most afraid of becoming like? Write about the traits in yourself that worry you, that you try to hide from others and especially yourself.

4. Write about the facade or mask you wear in the world—your public face. If the public could really know you, what would they know about you?

5. If you find yourself in a situation where it is difficult to speak your truths, create a fictional character and write a dialogue where the character speaks those same truths.

6. Write your response to the following quote by Henry Louis Mencken: *It is hard to believe that a man is telling the truth when you know that you would lie if you were in his place.* In what kinds of situations do you lie? And how do your justify your deceit?

7. Complete the following sentence: *I know I am being honest with myself when ...*

Exploring Joy

Sometimes your joy is the source of your smile, but sometimes your smile can be the source of your joy.

~ Thich Nhat Hanh

Joy, like happiness and pleasure, is something we all seek to some extent. We can feel joy over small occurrences—the smell of a flower, the feel of a summer breeze—and over large events—a wedding or the birth of a child.

Some people believe joy is a result of the right life circumstances, the number of "good" things that happen to you simply a matter of luck. Others believe it is a matter of choice or a spiritual practice. Still others think that a tendency to experience joy is a function of temperament, more than anything else.

Frequently, our journals reflect pain, problems, and anxieties. This week, take a time-out from worry; instead, take time to explore what makes you joyful.

This Week's Writing Prompts

1. What does "joy" mean to you? How is it different than "happiness" or "fun?"

2. Do a word association exercise with the word joy. Look over the list of words. Are there predominant themes, images, or memories? What do you notice about the list as a whole?

3. When you were a child, what gave you the most joy? Write about a time you remember feeling joyful.

4. As an adult, what gives you the most joy? Write about a recent time when you felt joyful. If you can't remember feeling joyful recently, write about how that feels.

5. Do you have enough joy in your life right now? Write about all the ways you have created joy in your life. Write about ways that you could create more joy in your life.

6. Think back to prompt number 3—what gave you joy as a child. This week do one thing associated with that same kind of joy. For example, if playing in the mud gave you joy, play in the mud—or clay—or Play-Doh. Then write about the experience. What happened? What did it bring up for you? What did you find out about yourself?

7. Make a list of three people you are close to. For each of those three people, list three things that you think bring them joy. Select one thing to do for one of those people this week—something simple. Then, write about what happened. Did the person react the way you anticipated? How did their response make you feel?

In Pursuit of Happiness

The care of human life and happiness, and not their destruction, is the first and only object of good government.

~ Thomas Jefferson

The U.S. constitution acknowledges our basic right to pursue happiness. And so we do. But happiness seems to be an elusive prize: each time we believe we've attained it, it slips from our grasp once again. This may be, in part, because we're not exactly sure what happiness is.

So what is happiness? According to my computer's dictionary, it is a feeling of pleasure or contentment; having a sense of confidence in or satisfaction with a person, arrangement, or situation; satisfied with the quality or standard of [something]. Synonyms include contentment, pleasure, satisfaction, cheerfulness, joy, joyfulness, delight, lightheartedness, well-being, rapture, bliss, and euphoria.

The Dalai Lama says, "The very purpose of life is to be happy." But, when our understanding of happiness includes everything from simple pleasure to rapture—all of which are temporary, as is the nature of feelings in general—how is a person to know when he's truly happy? And is it a state that can be attained and sustained?

This week's writing prompts

1. Turn on some quiet instrumental music and free write for ten minutes about what happiness means to you.

2. In what ways do you pursue happiness in your life: what methods do you use and/or actions do you take? What are the results of your efforts?

3. My mother used to say that happiness is overrated. She preferred, instead, the adrenaline rush of anxiety because it spurred to her new discoveries and achievements. What do you think about that attitude. Does it have merit? Why or why not?

4. Do you consider yourself a happy or unhappy person by nature? Another way of asking the question is, what is your default state? One of relative contentment and happiness, or one of discontent and unhappiness? Are you a "glass half-full" or a "glass half-empty" kind of person? Whatever your answer, explore in writing the reasons you categorize yourself that way. List evidence of your "natural" state and how it affects your general approach to life.

5. Write about the following quotes. How do you feel after reading each one? Other thoughts?

    The reason people find it so hard to be happy is that they always see the past better than it was, the present worse than it is, and the future less resolved than it will be. ~ Marcel Pagnol, French writer, producer and film director.

    If you want to live a happy life, tie it to a goal, not to people or things. ~ Albert Einstein.

Don't rely on someone else for your happiness and self worth. Only you can be responsible for that. If you can't love and respect yourself—no one else will be able to make that happen. Accept who you are—completely; the good and the bad—and make changes as YOU see fit—not because you think someone else wants you to be different. ~ Stacey Charter, cancer survivor.

6. Some people say that happiness is relative and that without the contrast to pain and discontent, pleasure and contentment have no meaning. Have difficult periods of your life enhanced your sense of joy and pleasure during the "up" times? If so, how. If not, why not?

7. What factors most influence your sense of happiness? And do you think that expectations play a role?

FAMILY & RELATIONSHIPS

FRIENDSHIP

It takes a long time to grow an old friend.

~ John Leonard

Most of us have strong beliefs about what friendships are all about, yet we don't examine the assumptions underlying those beliefs. Not that there's anything wrong with assumptions—it's just wise to be aware of when and where we hold them. It's wise, because not everyone believes the same things, and differences in belief systems are often a source of misunderstandings.

For example, if you believe a true friend should always be there for you when you need her, and a friend is unable to meet your expectation, you may feel hurt or betrayed. Your friend, on the other hand, may have felt that what you asked was beyond what she could do and you should have known that. She, then, reacts defensively to your expression of hurt, and ... well ... the rest is history.

Assumptions can be difficult to uncover because they lie beneath the surface of our conscious awareness. The following prompts are designed to help reveal and increase awareness of your assumptions and belief systems regarding the complicated topic of friendship.

This week's writing prompts

1. Complete the following statement: *A true friend is ...* Explain why your statement is true. When might it not be true?

2. Write about the sources of your beliefs about friendship: family of origin, experiences as a child, religious beliefs, literature, anything you can think of that has helped to form your beliefs.

3. How important are friends in your life, and in what ways have they influenced you, positively or negatively?

4. Many people believe that lasting friendships occur with a balance of intimacy and distance. Write about what you feel is the "right" amount of intimacy and what is the "right" amount of distance. Who in your life has fulfilled this balance and who has not? What do you perceive to be the differences in their personalities and approaches to life? How are their personalities and approaches similar or dissimilar to yours?

5. Do you agree or disagree with the following statement: "I have a lot of good friends whom I can depend on in time of need." Free write for ten minutes about your response.

6. In what ways are your adult friendships different than friendships you had as a child? In what ways are they the same?

7. If you could do life over again, would you do anything different in terms of your friendships and/or the effort you apply to friendships? Write about the reasons for your answer.

FAMILY CRISES

Family traditions counter alienation and confusion. They help us define who we are; they provide something steady, reliable and safe in a confusing world.

~ Susan Lieberman

Everyone experiences family crises from time to time, because we all have had families at some point in our lives. Family crises are such universal experiences that we create comedies with a family crisis as the central theme (think "Home for the Holidays") and satirize them on Hallmark cards. But a family crisis is not a pleasant experience when we're in the middle of it. Nothing seems funny or lighthearted and we wish it would just go away.

A crisis, by definition, is a turning point. It is the climax of a story, when something will either get easier or more difficult. Many things can precipitate a family crisis: traumatic events, such as unemployment, homelessness, drug use, marital problems, and illness, or everyday difficulties, such as habits or personality differences between family members. Whatever the cause, a crisis is stressful for everyone involved.

A crisis brings both danger and opportunity with it. There is danger of hurting someone and of making a situation worse. But there is also opportunity for healing and reconciliation. It can be difficult to recognize the gift in a crisis when you're smack dab in the middle of one, yet gifts exist, if we will only look for them.

A healthy way to help process feelings and thoughts—and to let off steam—during and after a time of crisis is to write about it. The following prompts will help you reflect on how you see yourself in your family, whether the family of your birth or the family with which you currently live—your roles, responsibilities, and reactions when crises occur.

This Week's Writing Prompts

1. Write down five words that describe your attitude toward your family of birth. Then expand on that by writing a paragraph for each word.

2. How do you see your role in your family? Do you play the role of family caretaker? Or perhaps you're an instigator? Write about your role and your feelings about it. Do you wish things were different? If so, describe how family life would be if you had your way.

3. Write about the last crisis in your family, in whatever ways you want to define family and crisis. What happened? Who was involved? What did you do or not do? Write about your feelings and what you think the feelings of others might have been. How did it turn out? Did you learn anything? Did anything positive come out of the situation?

4. In general, how do you cope with stressful family situations? Do you look for healing solutions or do you avoid them? Do you access external resources, such as therapy or do you feel you can handle things on your own? What kinds of feelings arise when you think about crisis in general?

5. In your family, what needs healing? Write about why you believe this.

6. Complete the following sentence: *The last time my family experienced a crisis, I thought ...*

7. Complete the following sentences:

   I think the most common sources of tension in my family are ...

   When I think about these sources of tension, I ....

Validating Love

We live by encouragement and die without it—slowly, sadly, angrily.

~ Celeste Holm

A friend once told me that the secret to lasting romance is to find out what the other person wants and give it to him or her; when both people in a relationship do this, their mutual desires are fulfilled.

Another secret (*why* are these secrets?) is to validate your lover's feelings and efforts on a daily basis. Simply thanking your partner for doing the dishes, the shopping, helping to make the bed, mow the lawn, and for working so hard to make life easier can go a long way.

Imagine being told every day that you're desirable, intelligent, and a worthy partner. Imagine being thanked for your efforts and your love. Imagine being told that your feelings matter, even when you're grumpy or irritable. Imagine how you would feel.

Now, imagine doing this for your loved ones.

Imagine validating your partner or lover, parents, children, and friends by letting them know how much you appreciate them. Every day.

Imagine what a world this could be.

This week's writing prompts:

1. Write about three people you love. For each person, list five things about him, or her, that he does well and that you admire. Make a point of validating all three people today by telling them what you wrote.

2. As an experiment this week, make a point of complimenting (validating) at least one person per day. At the end of the week, write for ten minutes about this experiment. Did you do it? If so, how did it feel? If not, write about what held you back and how you feel about it.

3. What does it mean to love someone? What does it mean to accept a person as she is? Are these the same things or different? How?

4. Write down 3-5 things that you do well or that you like about yourself. Stand in front of a mirror and say them to yourself. Yeah, you'll feel silly, but then you'll feel good!

5. Write for ten minutes about what it means to be affectionate and how you feel about affection in general. Was your family of origin affectionate or not, and how does that affect how you feel about the subject and/or your relationships with others?

6. Write about healthy and unhealthy relationships you've had, and the differences and similarities between them. What, in your opinion, makes a relationship stronger and healthier?

7. A while back, I came across a YouTube video titled "Validation." Watch the video (it's sixteen minutes long and well worth the time), then free write for ten minutes about your response.

   Here's the link: Validation
   (http://www.youtube.com/watch?v=Cbk980jV7Ao)

VULNERABILITY

There can be no vulnerability without risk; there can be no community without vulnerability; there can be no peace, and ultimately no life, without community.

~ M. Scott Peck

For most people, to be vulnerable means to be open to the possibility of physical or emotional injury, or easy manipulation, and is therefore a state we have learned to avoid. To protect ourselves, we build carefully contrived external personas and avoid letting down our guard for fear of being hurt emotionally, hiding those things about which we feel ashamed. We are afraid of being vulnerable because of the possibility of pain.

On the other hand, vulnerability also embodies hope—we are not yet hurt, and there is still the possibility of kindness.

I used to work for a non-profit organization called Challenge Day that facilitates experiential workshops for teens. During those workshops the teens and their adult counterparts experience increased human connection and trust by allowing themselves to be vulnerable with one another. They learn that, though our situations are different, we all experience the same kinds of hopes, fears, dreams, and disappointments. They learn that thinking you are the only person to feel a certain way (ashamed, hurt, fearful) is a common misconception. In the process of allowing themselves to be vulnerable, they no longer feel so alone.

What is your relationship to vulnerability and what do you understand its edges—its disadvantages and benefits—to be? What can you learn about yourself by exploring your feelings and thoughts about vulnerability?

This Week's Writing Prompts

1. Do a word association exercise with *vulnerable*. When you're done, review the list. What kinds of interesting associations occur? Are there any patterns that emerge? What can you learn about yourself from this exercise?

2. Free write for ten minutes about what it means for you to feel vulnerable.

3. When did you feel most vulnerable in your life? What happened? Was it a negative or positive experience, and how did it affect your responses to vulnerability afterwards?

4. Under what circumstances do you feel least vulnerable— most fortified, strong, and invulnerable? Do you feel more or less connected to others when you are least vulnerable? Free write for ten minutes about your answer.

5. Make a list of as many kinds of vulnerability as you can (interpret "kinds" any way you wish). Which of these kinds of vulnerability has the most emotional charge for you—

seems most important, urgent, critical, or increases
emotional sensations in your body—and in what ways?

6.   Generally speaking, how do you react to vulnerability in
     others? Do you want to protect them? Do you shy away
     from them (fear by association)? Do you find yourself
     hurting them? Explore, in writing, the sources of your
     reactions.

7.   Respond to the following quote by Anne Morrow
     Lindbergh: *I do not believe that sheer suffering teaches. If
     suffering alone taught, all the world would be wise, since
     everyone suffers. To suffering must be added mourning,
     understanding, patience, love, openness and the willingness to
     remain vulnerable.* Why might it be advantageous to be
     open and willing to remain vulnerable?

It's the Money, Honey

Money is better than poverty, if only for financial reasons.
~ Woody Allen

Just about everyone knows, or has heard, that how we handle money issues can make or break relationships. In fact, according to John Thyden, a Washington, D.C., divorce attorney, financial issues are the cause of 90 percent of divorce cases. Yet, while much has been written about how to overcome or deal with differences in the ways we handle money, rarely do we examine and clarify our own financial values. If we don't understand our own values—including their sources, benefits, and drawbacks—how can we expect to understand our partner's?

This week's prompts help you explore your money issues and values, and in what ways they impact your life.

This week's writing prompts

1. What is your first memory about money? What happened and why do you remember it? Which images evoke the strongest emotion?

2. List at least five things you remember hearing your parents say about money. Now list at least five things you remember about the way they handled money. Were their actions consistent with their words?

3. Did your parents tend to agree or disagree with each other when it came to money issues? What was your reaction to their lessons? Which values did you internalize and which did you rebel against? How has that internalization or rebellion created tension about money in your life?

4. What do you believe about money? Do you believe that it's hard to come by? Are you comfortable or uncomfortable with the idea of earning a lot of money? Do you feel deserving or undeserving when it comes to financial abundance? Do you resent those who have it? Free write for ten minutes about your attitudes about money. What, if anything, did you learn or notice about yourself as a result of your writing exploration?

5. How would you like to feel about money? Write a letter to Money, as if Money were a person, telling him or her what kind of relationship you would like to have.

6. When you think about discussing money with your partner or someone close to you, what are your dominant emotions? Shame? Anger? Anxiety? Satisfaction? Comfort? Name your emotions and then write about the money memories associated with them.

7. Have fun with this one: If you were to suddenly receive 10 million dollars, and you had to spend it and/or invest it within 24 hours, what would you do with it? Be specific: if you plan to invest a portion of it, exactly where would you invest it? If you want to give some of it away, exactly to whom or what organization(s) would you give it? Account for every penny.

PARENTS AND GROWN CHILDREN

Growing up human is uniquely a matter of social relations rather than biology. What we learn from connections within the family takes the place of instincts that program the behavior of animals; which raises the question, how good are these connections?

~ Elizabeth Janeway

Most of you reading this book are grown-ups, parents of grown-ups, or both. The parent-child bond is especially complicated by its never-ending quality: at sixty, you're still the child of your eighty-year-old parents. And, though these relationships occur in less-intimate quarters than when you were a child, as most grown-ups don't live with their parents, the quality of your relationships doesn't usually change all that much. If you had a combative relationship with your parents when you were young, that dynamic is often still in play when you get older. If your children tended to be overly dependent or too distant in their teens and early twenties, it's likely that not much has changed.

These things are true for all of us, yet how often do we explore our own roles in these relationship dynamics?

This week's writing prompts

1. Make a list of 10 similarities between you and your parents. If you have grown children, make separate lists of similarities between you and each of your children. Try to consider things you might not have thought about before. For example, examining photos of my mother and myself, I discovered—to my great surprise, since I had always thought our features quite different—that our eyes were identical in shape. This realization caused me to discover other similarities I had never considered before.

2. What, in your opinion are your parents' best and worst qualities, and why do you consider them so? Likewise, what are your children's best and worst qualities and why?

3. Since we cannot recognize qualities in others that we do not also have within us to varying degrees, write about how your parents' and/or children's best and worst qualities manifest themselves in you: how have they shown up in your life? Do you struggle with them? What would happen if you made peace with those qualities in yourself?

4. If appropriate to your situation, free write for ten minutes about what it means to be a grown child. Then, free write for ten minutes about what it means to be a parent of grown children.

5. Describe your ideal relationship with your parents. Now, describe your ideal relationship with your grown children. Where are the correlations between these two types of relationships? Do you expect different things of parents and children?

6. Thinking about the ideal relationships you wrote about in response to the previous prompt, if you could do anything differently in your relationships with your parents and your grown children, what would it be?

7. What do you think of the following quote by the psychiatrist, Thomas Szasz? *In the United States today, there is a pervasive tendency to treat children as adults, and adults as children. The options of children are thus steadily expanded, while those of adults are progressively constricted. The result is unruly children and childish adults.* Do you agree or disagree and why? If you agree, what has your role been in this scenario?

A JOURNAL WRITING COMMUNITY

*One definition of eternity is that we are not alone on this planet,
that there are those who've gone before and those who will come,
and that there is a community of spirits.*

~ Rita Dove

Writing can be a lonely, isolated way of life; this is
increasingly true as writers shift to working online. Even
writing teachers and editors like myself—who have
traditionally worked with other people—do much of our work
online. How do we know if our balance of writing life and
community is sufficient? And how do we create community
and support for our journaling and writing lives?

These questions are on my mind because Sunday afternoon
I attended a meeting of my local writing club. Each month the
club's program director brings in authors and/or members of
the publishing world to inspire us to believe in ourselves and to
persevere—whatever dire predictions have come our way—to
continue to write, learn, and grow. Even when I learn nothing
particularly new, I always come away from these meetings
feeling intellectually stimulated and connected to other writers.

This week's writing prompts

1. In general, would you describe yourself as a person who networks and builds a "support community," however you want to define the term, social or otherwise? In what ways yes and in what ways no? How important is it to you to have a support community?

2. As a journal-keeper and writer, do you think of yourself as isolated, engaged with other like-minded writers, or somewhere in between? Free write for ten minutes about where you see yourself on this spectrum and why.

3. Are you satisfied with your current writing community? Why or why not?

4. If you have a writing community to which you belong—a critique group, writer's club, writing circle—write about your role in these groups. Are you actively or passively engaged? Describe what you mean by your answer. If you don't have a writing community, write about the reasons and/or obstacles to having one.

5. How much time each day, on average, do you spend involved in online networking and how much time in real-time (person-to-person) networking? Do you feel satisfied with your investment of time, and what kinds of relationships, if any, have you developed each way?

6. Describe your ideal writing community. What would it look like, how much time would you spend interacting with other writers, and what kinds of interactions would you have? What do you bring to the community?

7. Regarding your current writing community, however small or large it is, make a list of then things you're grateful for. Then, make a list of five things you can do to strengthen

or enlarge your support community. And if you're already happy with the community that you've developed, make a list of five more things you can contribute to it.

OBSTACLES & OPPORTUNITIES

WHEN DESIRE AND REALITY COLLIDE

There are two tragedies in Life. One is not to get your heart's desire. The other is to get it.

~ George Bernard Shaw

I once went to a strobe lighting seminar in Sacramento, taught by Joe McNally, the all-time portrait lighting guru. The seminar was fast-paced, comprehensive, and entertaining. And it made me want things: more speedlights, those special C-stands, and all those diffusion and reflection devices; backgrounds and frames; a photography studio; assistants; and photography jobs that would pay me more money than all that stuff would cost.

But I didn't stop there. My desires spread uncontrollably like an oil spill in the gulf coast. I wanted the new version of Photoshop (CS5) so badly, I could taste and smell the hours I'd put in at the computer learning all the cool new features. What if I bought the whole master suite? It cost, at the time, about $1,800 dollars, but because I was taking a class at the community college, I could get it for the student price of $525. Of course, that was $525 I didn't have.

Prior to the seminar, I bought two new purses so that I could carry my iPad with me wherever I went. Because I had a new iPad, I also had to buy essential accessories and cables to go with it. A cover. Several new apps. E-books.

I had no idea how much I'd spent, and was afraid to look at my credit card balance. The disparity between the reality of my financial life and my lust for all this software and hardware—tools for creativity—caused the muscles around my spleen to clench.

My fingers hovered over the Add to Shopping Cart button for the 15th time. I wanted to push that button. I wanted to own those things, to have them at my disposal. But I knew I couldn't justify the expense. Like a tethered animal desiring a treat or a water bowl that has been placed just out of reach, I strained at the end of my rope, frustrated and whining. (All this happens internally, of course. My family would think I'd finally flipped if I had actually been whining.)

What could I do? I wrote. I put down these feelings, named the desire for what it was—techno-lust. I brought it to its proper place in the larger perspective of my life. Those things were, in truth, not that important. I told myself I could have everything I wanted, but that I had to wait for some things. I needed to think about my true priorities in life, like connecting with people, writing, and actually taking pictures. Truly, I had everything I needed.

As I wrote, I calmed down. The seemingly uncontrollable yearning, the whining animal at the end of its rope, circled near its post and lay down, panting.

Writing is a tool we always have at our disposal. It costs nothing but time and energy. And the very act of bringing thoughts, feelings, and desires to the light of the page, enacts a welcome clarity of vision and healing.

It also allows us to see ourselves as part of the larger community of writers. I know that we all struggle with wanting things, or people, that we can't have—at least not when we want them. So this week's topic is When Desire and Reality Collide.

This Week's Writing Prompts

1. What do you desire to have in your life right now? Is it a thing, an event, a job, a person? Write about what you want. Describe it in great detail. Describe what you imagine would happen if you had this thing or job or person in your life.

2. In the novel written by Miguel De Cervantes, Don Quixote says, "I would do what I please, and doing what I pleased, I should have my will, and having my will, I should be contented; and when one is contented, there is no more to be desired; and when there is not more to be desired, there is an end of it." How do you feel when you read these words? What is your immediate reaction? Explore that reaction: what are its roots? Is your reaction related to things you were taught as a child by your parents or other family members?

3. Do you have judgments about your desires and wants? Do you think that you shouldn't want whatever it is that you desire? Or do you think that it is perfectly natural? Write

the ideas, the ideals and principles behind your feelings. How do these ideals affect your general outlook on life?

4. Napoleon Hill said, "Desire is the starting point of all achievement, not a hope, not a wish, but a keen pulsating desire which transcends everything." Everything we desire has an underlying attachment to an end goal of some kind. Is your desire something that drives you, that gives you focus? Is your desire related to achievement? How or how not?

5. Imagine that you have achieved your desire and that you are standing in that place of accomplishment. Now, write a conversation between that you, and the current you. What advice does the "accomplished you" give the "current you"?

6. When you want something that costs more money or time than you have, what do you do? Do you buy it anyway, on credit? Do you spend the time working on getting it, at the expense of other commitments and responsibilities? Do you save up the money? Work the time into your schedule? Or, at the other end of the spectrum, do you tell yourself you can't have whatever it is and try to suppress the desire? Write about your response and your feelings about it. Do you think you respond differently than you do?

7. What do you think life would be like if you could have everything you wanted, whenever you wanted it?

Overcoming Obstacles

Conquering any difficulty always gives one a secret joy, for it means pushing back a boundary-line and adding to one's liberty.
~ Henri Frederic Ariel, Author

I was in the car with my teenage son, discussing the documents we needed in order to open his first bank account. The conversation went something like this:

Me: Where's your social security card?

Him: I gave it back to you, clipped to that folder.

Me: What folder?

Him: Mom, I don't want to talk about it now.

Me: Well, when will we talk about it?

Him: I don't know. I feel like you're grilling me.

Me: I just want to understand what you mean. What folder?

Him: It doesn't matter.

Me: Yes it does. Don't you want to remember where it is? That's a pretty important document.

Him: I don't care. There's nothing I can do about it right now, anyway.

Me: Yes there is. You could remember where you put it so that you have it when you need it.

Him: I don't want to talk about it now.

Me: When you have something you need to remember or need to figure out, don't you just want to keep thinking about it until you solve the problem?

Him: No. I don't want to think about it until I have to think about.

Me: Well, I guess that's one of our differences. When it comes to problem solving, I'm like a dog with a bone—I just won't let go until I have the answer.

Him: Whatever.

The conversation made me think about the different problem solving styles we each have. My son is a class procrastinator "I'll think about it when I have to...." I'm a type-A problem solver and workaholic who gets so focused that my family sometimes has to yell that the house is on fire to get my attention. (I made up that last part, but you know what I mean.)

How we choose to solve problems or overcome perceived obstacles is an important aspect of our individual expressions of creativity. The following writing prompts will help you to explore your responses to obstacles and the ways in which you go about solving challenges.

This Week's Writing Prompts

1. How would you describe your general response to problems? Are you action-oriented, trusting your instincts and intuition to lead you to the right solutions? Or do you like to consider all sides of an issue, figure out what

resources are available to you, and only then choose a direction to take? Do you fall somewhere in-between these two extremes? Or do you avoid problem solving all together? Free write for ten minutes in response to these questions.

2. Finish the following sentence: *The last time I encountered an obstacle, I...* What was the result of your action or inaction?

3. List three things that you would like improved in your life. Then, close your eyes, breathe deeply, and imagine each of those improvements as if they were already a reality. Do this for ten to twenty long, slow breaths. How do you feel? Spend ten minutes writing about the feelings you experienced as you imagined having those improvements in place. Now, for each item, list three possible ways of achieving that improvement. Write down the first three things that pop into your mind, without judgment or worrying about how "realistic" those ways might be.

4. Perform a word association with the word *problem*. Keep pushing for words, even repeat words if that's what comes to mind, until your mind is blank. When you're done writing words, take a look at what you've written. What do these words and images tell you about your core attitudes and beliefs about problems?

5. Finish the following sentences:

    I feel most effective as a problem solver when ...

    I feel the least effective as a problem solver when ...

6. Do you agree with the following statement? "There is a way around, over, or through every obstacle in life." Whatever your answer, why do you think you believe it?

Where did you first hear or see that attitude? What occurred that encouraged you to internalize that belief?

7. List three obstacles you have overcome or problems you have solved, where you felt proud of yourself afterward. Write a scene about one of those times. Include setting and dialogue if possible.

SAYING YES

Opportunity is often dressed up in work clothes.

~ Croft M. Pentz

Sometimes, Opportunity comes knocking, but she's disguised as something that will require time every weekend or once a month on Tuesday evenings when we'd much rather be sitting on the couch watching "Lost." So we hurriedly slam the door in Opportunity's face, because we're afraid that she's really a giant, time-sucking sinkhole in disguise: that thing we said yes to but then wished we hadn't, because it really hasn't turned out the way we thought, and now we're not getting done what we really need to get done.

It's true: those nasty time-sucking sinkholes can creep up on you when you least expect it. Especially if you're a person who hasn't built healthy boundaries and who has a tendency to say yes too often. You do need to be careful. Still, what if you slam the door on Opportunity, and she gets angry and refuses to visit for a long time after that? What if that was only the first of many times she would have come your way if you had, indeed, said yes?

When I ask successful writers, artists, and entrepreneurs what they believe is the most important reason for their success—in addition to hard work—they always cite "saying yes to every opportunity." By looking for and remaining receptive to opportunities, door after door seemed to almost magically open in front of them. They usually go on to add that at the time, they didn't realize where these opportunities would lead. In retrospect, they see how, by working hard and saying yes to the small opportunities, they built, step by step, the stairs that led them to the success they enjoy today. The thing is, they continue to say yes to opportunities.

"But what about those nasty sinkholes?" you might ask. Here's the thing: Opportunities that are true opportunities give something back to us immediately; we enjoy that activity, make money doing it, or are fed by it in some other way. Sinkholes, on the other hand, usually lead us on by promising a reward of some kind, and then fail to pay on those promises. And, nine times out of ten, we feel immediately that we've made a mistake.

This is where having healthy boundaries come into play. Because, although sinkholes work hard to make you believe that you can't change your mind once you've said yes, they are actually quite shallow. Once you realize that the activity is not rewarding to you, you can change your mind and walk away. Yes, you can.

This Week's Writing Prompts

1. Without consulting the dictionary, define the word *opportunity*. What does it mean to you personally? Have you had a lot of opportunities in life, or just a few?

2. What is your general attitude toward opportunities? Do you think they'll come looking for you, or do you have to make them happen?

3. When you say yes to something that ends up feeling unrewarding, do you feel free to change your mind and say no, or do you feel stuck with you initial commitment? What are the underlying beliefs for your actions?

4. Think about the requests for help, expertise, or time that have come your way in the last few weeks or months. What have you said no to that could have been an opportunity in disguise? Write about what influenced your decision at the time.

5. Write down two goals for the next year. Make a list of several, small actions that could lead to increased opportunities. Stuck for ideas? Write about what it would be like to be unstuck.

6. Write the word *Yes* in the center of a blank page and draw a circle around it. Close your eyes, take two deep breaths, open them, and look at the word. Write down the first word or draw the first image that comes into your mind. Keep writing/drawing until your mind is quiet. Review the associations you made. What do these tell you about your belief systems and ways of thinking?

7. Say yes to everything that comes your way this week—on condition that you can change your mind at the last minute if you choose to do so. Write about how you feel now, at the beginning of the week. At the end of the week, write about what happened.

SAYING NO

Risk! Risk anything! Care no more for the opinions of others, for those voices. Do the hardest thing on earth for you. Act for yourself. Face the truth.

~ Katherine Mansfield

We have practiced saying yes to opportunities and to life, expanding our horizons and looking beyond our fears. This week, we will explore what it means to say no. The kind of no I'm talking about is a healthy no, a considered no, a no that comes from the gut, a no that says, "this won't work for me right now." It's not an absolute, forever no, but a clear and temporal no. It's not a no that comes from fear, but a no that comes from love—of ourselves.

There are a host of reasons why we might have a difficult time refusing a request. Many of us were raised to feel responsible for others' feelings and to act in ways that would please them, even at our own expense. We were taught to say yes to requests, even when we had personal reservations, in order to make other people happy. In my case, as a child and young adult, I wanted so badly to be loved and accepted that I would do things that weren't in my own best interests in order to win the approval of others. Over time, I learned that I wasn't doing anyone a favor by agreeing to something because of external pressure, a sense of obligation, or simply because I didn't value my own feelings about the issue.

No can be a difficult thing to say. What's it been like for you?

This Week's Writing Prompts

1. How does saying no sit with you? In general, do you have an easy or difficult time saying no to others? What factors in your life contributed to this ease or difficulty? For example, when you were growing up, were your feelings and responses acknowledged and respected? Or were you taught to always try to be polite and make other people happy, even if it meant stuffing your own feelings? Is it really okay to say no to someone?

2. Complete the following sentence: *Every time I say no, I risk ...*

3. Complete the following sentence: *Every time I don't say no when I think I should, I risk ...*

4. Write about he last time you said no to a request or a project. Describe the scene as vividly as possible: where were you and what was going on around you? Who was involved? Use dialogue. What prompted you to refuse the request and how did it turn out?

5. Think about a time when you really felt you should say no, but the person requesting pleaded and pushed and cajoled you into saying yes. What happened? Now, rewrite history by rewriting the entire event, this time saying no clearly, calmly, and decisively. Create a story about what happens. How do you feel?

6. Do you often feel overcommitted, stressed, and/or overwhelmed? Is saying yes a pattern in your life? Write a fictional story about your life in which you say no to everything you don't want to do. Be creative. What is this fictional life like? What happens? How do you feel after you write the story?

7. This week, experiment with saying no. For each request that comes your way, respond, "Let me think about it," even if it's something you want to do. Then, take time to look at your schedule, your current list of commitments, and make a considered decision. If it's something you truly want to do, but realize that you don't have time, either remove something else to make room for this new commitment or negotiate to start later, when you have more time. If you find, after thinking about it, that you feel any reluctance or doubt about the request, turn it down.

THE PROBLEM OF TIME

There is a time for everything, and a season for every activity under the heavens.

~ Ecclesiastes 3:1

We all know about time. We live in it, through it, use it, and waste it. It flies and flows, speeds up, and slows down. We create philosophies, sciences, and art in our attempts to understand it. And we argue about it. When we're engaged in activities we enjoy, time seems to pass quickly, but when we're engaged in something we don't want do, or are waiting for the proverbial water to boil, time seems to pass as slowly as diamonds emerging from carbon. Our perception of time is influenced both by our personalities and by external factors; some people always seem to be in a hurry while others do not. But, no matter how we think about time, we are in agreement on one thing: there is never enough of it.

When I have insufficient time to complete a task, I feel stressed. My chest constricts. I can't catch a full breath. panic ensues, as though my life is packed into a container that is too small. Time is the container, and somehow I have to fit everything into it or … what? I will fail, I will die, something will go terribly wrong. These are the mad thoughts I associate with a shortage of time.

But I can shift those feelings by changing my metaphor for time. Rather than a container, I could picture time as something fluid and without boundaries, as a river of energy, for example. It then becomes the environment in which I swim, instead of a box that holds me in. Because it is fluid, it never ends. It expands and contracts according to the channel that it carves out of the surrounding landscape. This time, in my imagination, is a broad river, wide and strong and true. Within this river, I flow, connecting with other people and things along the way. Ahhh ... conceptualizing time this way helps me to feel so much better!

But sometimes rivers rush quickly and there are rapids. The idea of being caught in the rapids is scary. So, let's go back to the original metaphor of time as a container. Only now, I'll imagine it as a container that is so large, I can live in it, with walls so far away, I cannot see them. I can't even find them. The container is limitless and, like the universe, it's constantly in a state of expansion. Time, therefore, has no solid boundary, even though it is a container in which I live.

If I then picture a day—24 hours—as a portion of this limitless container, a portion that I am free to fill with activities and thoughts, I can also imagine that everything I do is a contribution to the expansion of the universe. I feel calmer already!

Consider these additional metaphors for time:

- Time is an onion, except instead of peeling layers away, each moment adds, layer by layer to the onion.

- Time is the foundation of a house on which we build, room by room.

- Time is a gift. We unwrap it and discover its wonders, like a toy with never-ending possibilities for play.

This Week's Writing Prompts

1. How do you usually feel about time? Does the thought of your day fill you with a high sense of urgency or a low one?

2. What do you remember your parents saying about time?

3. Create a new metaphor for Time by finishing the sentence, "Time is ..."

4. If I could change anything about time, it would be _____. Then, elaborate on what would happen if that change occurred.

5. If I could travel to a different time, I would travel to _____, because ...

6. Albert Einstein said that "The only reason for time is so that everything doesn't happen at once." What do you think about that sentiment? Do you think it's true? Why or why not?

7. Write about your reaction to the saying, "Don't count every hour in the day; make every hour in the day count."

PHYSICAL LIMITATIONS

The artist's world is limitless. It can be found anywhere, far from where he lives or a few feet away. It is always on his doorstep.

~ Paul Strand

Sometimes ill health or lack of physical abilities seems to get in the way of doing what we want to do. I write "seem" because I believe that how we respond to life's situations is more about our perceptions of reality than reality itself. Are restrictions truly limiting or are they only limiting because we perceive them as such?

Consider the 72-year-old who competes in Iron Man Triathlons, wheelchair-bound athletes who bicycle miles over steep mountain roads using their arms to propel them, deaf composer Ludwig Beethoven, and blind artist Eşref Armağan. Each of these extraordinary people has surmounted what most of us think of as an insurmountable limitation. They refused to accept the conventional view of their physical abilities and creatively approached what they wanted to accomplish.

Years ago, I discovered that when I gave students strict guidelines for assignments, they tended to return the most creative work. Whereas, when I left things wide open, they were less creative. This happened time and time again. I came to the conclusion that when we are restricted in some way, we must rely on our creativity to rise above what we may initially see as limitations in order to accomplish what we set out to do.

What has this got to do with journaling? This week's writing prompts will help you to explore the limiting circumstances in your life, your perceptions of your abilities, and new ways that you might approach those limitations.

This Week's Writing Prompts

1. Describe what being and feeling limited means to you.

2. If you could physically do anything you wanted (we're not talking superpowers here, just normal human physical abilities), what would you do and why?

3. Do you feel limited and/or held back in any way by a lack of physical ability or ill health? If so, write about the physical restriction. What does it keep you from doing that you could do otherwise?

4. Have there been times in your life when you felt restricted in some way—not necessarily physical— yet found a creative solution to overcome the restriction? Write about that time, the circumstances around the restriction, and how you arrived at your creative solution. How did/do you feel afterward? What is different now, if anything?

5. Think about the people who exceed their physical limitations, such as the athletes and artists in the second paragraph above. Do their examples inspire you? Why or why not? What, in particular, makes these people extraordinary? What do you think it takes to lift the ordinary into the extraordinary?

6. Make a list of at least five ways you could overcome your physical limitations. For each way, write down the reasons you would not be able to accomplish it. Now, argue with that reason: why is each reason an excuse?

7. What abilities do you have that some other people don't have? What can you do that they can't? How can you use your abilities to overcome your limitations?

GOING WITH THE FLOW

Relax Ride the wave. Go with the flow. Let go, let God. Surrender to what is. Breathe. Chill out. These are all the sorts of practical but infuriating things people say to you when you're stressed out or upset about something that is not going the way you wish. Maybe your boss asks you to work late way too often, your daughter is dating a guy you're afraid might lead her in an unhealthy direction, someone you love is sick, or no one is buying your photography. Whatever the reason, the bottom line is that you are not in control of the situation. You feel like you're riding the rapids, and your canoe is just about to tip.

But when there's nothing you can do about a situation, stress, frustration, and anger—though natural responses—are neither healthy nor productive. Of course knowing this does not make it any easier to let go of wanting control, of wanting the situation to be different. In spite of your best efforts to just "chill out," you find yourself gnawing the corners of your fingernails.

What do you do when there's nothing you can do?

Journal writing is not only a great way to process and work through emotion, it's also a good way to look at what's at the bottom of your resistance—what it is that you fear—and come to terms with a situation.

This Week's Writing Prompts

1. What are you resisting in your life right now (a change, someone else's behavior)? How does that resistance make you feel? Empowered or powerless? Frustrated or hopeful? Active of stifled?

2. Think about something you feel stressed or upset about and complete the following sentence as many times as possible, as quickly as possible: *I'm afraid that* ....

3. Write about a time when you tried to control something that was outside your ability to control. What was the result?

4. Make a list of everything you can think of over which you have no control. If it's easier, start with the large things—earthquakes, natural disasters, wars—and move to the small things. Include behaviors of others (my brother's smoking). Keep writing until you can't think of anything else. Then, look over the list and write about any connections, insights, or observations you make about it.

5. Think about the last time you felt upset. What was happening? What did you do or not do? What can you learn from that event?

6. Have you ever had a time when you were able to let go of wanting control and allow yourself to ride the wave of uncertainty? If no, why do you think that is, and if yes, what happened as a result?

7. Lao-Tzu is reputed to have said, "Life is a series of natural and spontaneous changes. Don't resist them—that only creates sorrow. Let reality be reality. Let things flow naturally forward in whatever way they like." Do you think resistance creates sorrow? If you wanted to, how could you reduce resistance to change? What would it take for you to sit back, relax, and go with the flow?

THE NATURE OF RESISTANCE

Resistance is thought transformed into feeling. Change the thought that creates the resistance, and there is no more resistance.

~ Robert Conklin

At its simplest, resistance is opposition: one force that opposes another force. The term is used to describe aspects of motion, politics, war, and bacteria. But this week, we're going to examine emotional resistance.

By emotional resistance, I mean that feeling of conflict that centers itself somewhere in your body—your gut or your throat, perhaps—when you feel obligated to do something you don't want to do. It may also arise when you feel off balance because of unwanted change or an unfamiliar occurrence. You may feel resistance from others when you present a new idea or ask them to change behaviors.

According to awareness gurus, the road to happiness and even enlightenment could be as simple as dropping resistance to whatever is happening in the moment—you might even resist the idea of giving up resistance!

It's a good idea to pay attention to feelings of resistance, because resistance nearly always signals an area in which a person needs to grow. When you acknowledge your resistance, rather than deny it, and examine reasons for that resistance, you'll always learn something new about yourself.

This Week's Writing Prompts

1. Think of the last time you felt resistance to something (it could be now). What was/is it—a change, a person, an idea? How do you know when you're resisting something? Where do you feel it in your body?

2. The last time you felt resistance, what did you do? Write about the situation, your response, and what happened.

3. Write about a time you worked through your resistance. What did you learn? For example, I had an assignment to write about something that felt overwhelming to me. I resisted it. Once I identified the reasons for my resistance, I understood that I had something to learn by tackling the assignment.

4. Write about a time you received resistance from someone else. What was the situation at the time? What did you do about it, and what happened?

5. Do a word association exercise with the word *resistance*. What patterns and/or feelings do you perceive in your list of words?

6. Write a short, non-fiction memoir (memory) or write a poem about resistance using words from your list.

7. Free write for ten minutes about the strategies you use when you want to overcome a feeling of resistance within yourself.

CONTROL

It isn't until you come to a spiritual understanding of who you are—not necessarily a religious feeling, but deep down, the spirit within—that you can begin to take control.

~ Oprah Winfrey

A recent health-related article stated that feelings of helplessness and lack of control are significant factors contributing to depression, particularly for women. As I read the article, I started to think about how important choice and control have been in my life. How, in fact, I have always demanded a certain level of decision-making authority in my jobs—or moved on. How, when I have felt most helpless, I have fought like crazy to gain control over any aspect, no matter how tiny, of the situation. Perhaps instinctively, I knew that to surrender to my sense of powerlessness would begin a downward emotional spiral.

Even in children, you can see how important choice is. A child, given no choice about whether to wear a particular shirt might throw a tantrum. But take that same shirt and offer the child a choice of a second shirt, and he may very well choose the one you wanted him to wear in the first place. The choice, not the shirt, is what your child wants. It's no different for adults. Choice and a sense of personal power go hand in hand.

Sometimes, in the thick of things—an embattled relationship, a job you don't like, a loss of some kind—it's difficult to see a way out or what can be done to ease feelings of stress, grief, and helplessness. But when we recognize that even allowing ourselves to feel and express anger is a way of taking control, we can understand that it doesn't take much to improve our sense of power.

Journal writing about a situation is a good way to take control over it. You get to define the situation in your own terms. You get to say what you do and don't like about it. You get to express your anger however you want: write in red, angry slashes on the page, draw angry pictures, and/or say hurtful things you wouldn't actually want to say to someone. Through the act of journaling, you get to clarify what's most important to you and create a plan for change.

Here are some suggestions for how to write through and about those situations in which you feel out of control.

This Week's Writing Prompts

1. Think about a current situation in which you have no control. Describe that situation as thoroughly as possible. Who's involved? How did you get here? What were your expectations for this situation, and how is reality different than those expectations?

2. What is the primary problem? Complete the following sentence: *I would feel better if only ...* Write the sentence as

many times as possible, each time expanding upon the answer before it.

3. If your responses to prompt number 2 were about someone else taking action, for instance, "I would feel better if only my husband/boss/son/job would ...," ask yourself what you would do to make *yourself* feel better. We can't control the actions and feelings of others; we can only control our own actions and feelings. Our helplessness stems from wanting someone else to change. Complete the following prompt: *I would feel better if only I could/would* ... Why would that action help you to feel better?

4. If your responses to prompt number 2 are about something you feel that you can't do, such as, "I would feel better if I could just quit my job and move to Hawaii," complete the following sentence: *The things that are keeping me from _____ are* ... Now, separately, for each of the things you listed as roadblocks, complete the following sentence: *I could do _____ if* ...

When you're done, look over what you've written. Are there any steps, however small, you could take toward any of those "if" answers? If so, write down what those might be and how you might go about doing them. How does thinking about these possibilities feel to you?

5. Thinking about the situation, respond to the following prompt: "If the situation doesn't change, I am afraid that ..." Next, whatever you answered, write, "I am afraid of _____ because ..." Continue to do this until you get down to the basic fear beneath your sense of helplessness. For example, I might write, "If the situation doesn't change, I'm afraid I'll lose my house." Next, "I am afraid of losing my house because I don't know where I'll live." I would start the next prompt, "I am afraid of not knowing where I'll live because ..." And so on.

6. Make a list of at least five positive aspects of your situation. Start with the first thing that pops into your mind. For example, if my situation is that my boss criticizes me constantly, I might start with: "I can learn from her criticism and improve my performance—even if she doesn't recognize it." List as many things as you can. Write about how you feel after making that list.

7. Write for at least ten minutes in response to the following quote by Brian Tracy (TV host): *You cannot control what happens to you, but you can control your attitude toward what happens to you, and in that, you will be mastering change rather than allowing it to master you.* Do you think what he says is true or not true? Why or why not? What could you change about your attitude towards your current situation?

SEASONS & HOLIDAYS

ENDINGS AND BEGINNINGS

Life is not so much about beginnings and endings as it is about going on and on and on. It is about muddling through the middle.

~ Anna Quindlen

Life is full of endings and beginnings, all bittersweet in their own ways. Perhaps that is why we so widely celebrate the turning of a calendar year. The date itself might be arbitrary, but the symbolic ending of the old and the beginning of the new is important.

Each year, it is tradition to take stock of the old year and look ahead to the coming one. Witness all the "Best of Year" "Top Ten," and "Top Ten Predictions" articles that are in all the newspapers, magazines, and blogs. While there is so much of this in the media we might be tempted to forego a personal version of the tradition, I believe that these are worthy exercises to undertake, especially for journal writers.

These prompts are designed to help you find your own way of celebrating and marking turning points in your life. You may choose to respond to these prompts at the beginning of a new calendar year, but you can also use them to mark the beginning of a personal year, such as your birthday or another personal anniversary of some kind.

Taking Stock of the Old

1. Make a list of the five or ten most exciting events that occurred the previous year. When the list is complete, go back and write a little more detail about each event. Why was it exciting? What importance did it have for you at the time and now? What significance might it have for the future?

2. What is the most important accomplishment you achieved?

3. What was your greatest failure and/or disappointment during the previous year and what did you, or could you, learn from the experience?

4. Make a list of new acquaintanceships and/or friendships that developed over the last year. Which of these relationships would you like to deepen more in the future and why?

5. If you wrote a letter to yourself at the beginning of last year (see prompt number 1 in the "Looking Forward to the New" section), read your letter and write about which parts of it came true and which didn't.

Looking Forward to the New

1. Write a letter to yourself making predictions about your life in the coming year.

2. What is the most important thing you'd like to achieve during the coming year (yes, just one!), and why?

3. What is your greatest fear about the coming year, and
    what steps can you take to overcome or take action in spite
    of that fear?

4. What kind of friendships would you like to develop or
    focus on this coming year? Who is in your life today that
    you want to get to know better? What clubs do you want
    to join? Make a list and then circle the three most likely to
    happen.

5. What group, local or international, would you most like to
    help this year and how? List ten different ways you could
    get involved.

6. Write a fictional conversation dated December 31st of the
    following year (for example, if this was 2011, you would
    date it 12/31/2012) in which you are the main character.
    In this story, you are having a conversation with your best
    friend about the previous year.

Pick at least one prompt from Taking Stock and Looking
Forward, and have fun!

SPRING

Break open a cherry tree and there are no flowers, but the spring breeze brings forth myriad blossoms.

~ Ikkyu Sojun

Spring is a time of transition between the old year and the new, when everything changes rapidly—growing, greening, budding, and flowering. Spring is also a symbol for certain life experiences: times of change, times of growth, times that vacillate between rain and sun, pessimism and hope. For all these reasons, spring is a wonderful catalyst for journal writing.

Personally, I love this time of year, when the ground brings forth bright surprises, and the grass, which has been hibernating all winter, begins to stretch itself toward the sun. I always feel a little as though I am waking up, unfolding from the earth, reaching up myself. As though the thoughts and feelings that have been hibernating all winter take root and begin to sprout. Then I understand that when I thought I was being unproductive, I was merely storing energy for a burst of growth.

This Week's Writing Prompts

1. Write about your very first spring memory. What about that memory gives you the best feelings? What about it gives you the worst feelings? What does that memory represent for you?

2. Perform a word association exercise with the word *spring*. When you are done, look over the list of words. Finish the following sentence: *When I read this list of words, I feel ... because ...*

3. The most common spring metaphors include the start of a period of growth, renewal, and better times. What other metaphors are true for you? Find out by completing this sentence in five different ways: In my life, spring is ...

4. What is your favorite spring flower? What color is it? Does that color show up in your life in other ways? If so, how does it show up? What emotions do you associate with that flower and/or that color?

5. Who in your family most reminds you of spring? Why?

6. If you could spend spring anywhere in the world, where would it be and why? What would you do while you were there? In what ways would that spring vacation renew your spirit?

7. How would you describe yourself emotionally, using spring weather as a metaphor? For example, I am mostly sunny with some clouds in the late afternoon. After you've described yourself, free write about that idea for ten minutes.

REMEMBERING SUMMERS

Ah, summer, what power you have to make us suffer and like it.

~ Russell Baker

The word *summer* carries its own set of images for each of us: family picnics, camping, hot hours in a car, iridescent heat waves rising from a road in midday, a mirage of distant water. Lakeside barbecues, tomatoes fresh from the vine, grilled corn. Heat. Water pistol wars. Popsicles. Heat.

During the summers of 2010 and 2011, the news was full of record-breaking temperatures pushing in waves through Europe and the U.S. There were pictures of children playing in water fountains in London and sunbathers in downtown Moscow. In Northern California, where I lived, it was hot—in the 90s—but not abnormally so. Just the usual dry heat of long summer days, when it's better to be indoors or sheltered by the shade. When romantic walks in the cool of the evening are welcomed. When bands play in the park on Friday nights.

What images does the word *summer* bring to your mind? Think about what you will do this summer and what you've done in past summers, as a child, a teenager, and so on ... all the memories. Let those images float through your mind. Are there any memories that seem more significant than others? Take those images and memories and dig a little deeper.

This Week's Writing Prompts

1. Jot down summaries of significant summer memories that come to mind. Now, select one of those memories and describe the scene in detail, including where you were, who you were with, what you did, the conversation, and so on.

2. Write about why that memory is significant. What happened that made it especially important to you? Did the event change you in any way? If so, how? Who were you before and after?

3. Think about the people who were present, if any. Do you still know any of them? Are they still significant in your life? If so, write about them and what their presence in that memory means to you. If there is no one but you in that memory, write about why that significant experience was solitary.

4. As you get older, how have summers and the activities you engage in changed? Is there anything you wish you could still do, but feel that you can't? Is there something you had forgotten about, but would like to do again? What was there about that activity that made it a fulfilling one?

5. On a piece of scrap paper, make a list of one-word images. Try to include both nouns and verbs in your list (tents, popsicles, sunbathing, beach, running, swimming, etc.). When you are done, cut out the individual words and rearrange in any way you like. Make a word collage for summer.

6. As a child, what was your favorite summer game? Describe the game and why you liked it so much. Does some remnant of that game still exist in your life? Why or why not? How do you feel about it?

7. Pick a five-year span of your life and try to remember every summer of that span. Write down what you did each summer, even if it was simply, "worked, didn't go on vacation, had a family barbecue for July 4th." Then, select one or more of those summers, and finish the following sentences:

   At the time, I wanted to ...

   That summer, the most wonderful thing was ...

   That summer, the most difficult thing was ...

   If I could go back and do it differently, I would ...

   I am so happy that ...

FROM ONE SEASON TO ANOTHER

The events of childhood do not pass, but repeat themselves like seasons of the year.

~ Eleanor Farjeon

Where I live, in Napa, California, the heat of summer arrived late, after months of unusually cool weather—ironic, considering that the calendar said we were officially entering the fall season. The day before, as we celebrated the birthday of my beloved with an outdoor barbecue and picnic, I reflected on the inexorable forward movement of the seasons, and how many memories are associated with each one.

Summer, for instance, is filled with childhood memories of camping, swimming, skateboarding, and running around the neighborhood with friends. One of my favorite childhood summer memories is of playing the old-fashioned game of Kick-the-Can in the streets of our neighborhood as twilight gave us relief from the oppressive heat of the day. And then there's autumn.

Some—those who don't live here—say that Northern California has only two seasons. I heartily disagree. In autumn, the leaves here turn orange and crimson and yellow and drift earthward, as wonderful for piling and jumping in as leaves anywhere else. Fall rains are often warm enough to enjoy without the cover of an umbrella, and the thrill of stomping through puddles never really disappears. Winter here is mild, but still creates longings for hibernation, warm fires, hot chocolate, slippers, and a good book. And, of course, spring brings that sense of awakening, fresh clean air, new life, and a desire to get out and see the new green world again.

I invite you to explore how the seasons have shaped your life with the following prompts.

This Week's Writing Prompts

1. What is one of your favorite childhood memories of summer? Why do you think of it so fondly, and who was there with you?

2. In what ways do you, as an adult, recreate those memories? (For example, if sitting around the campfire is one of your favorites, do you camp often? Take your family along?) And if you don't recreate them, why don't you? What holds you back?

3. When you think about the change of seasons, summer to fall in particular, what image comes to mind? Using colored pencils or crayons, draw your impression of that image. Even if you don't think of yourself as an "artist," this is great fun. And no one else needs to see it. Let the child in you come out to play!

4. Do you look forward to fall, or do you resist it? Explore your answer. What emotions do you associate with each of these seasons, and what memories go along with those

emotions? If you have any negative emotions towards a particular season, how could you rewrite the story of your life to create positive feelings towards that time of year?

5. Do a word association with the word *summer*. Now do a word association with the word *fall*. After you have completed both word association sessions, look over your list of words. Do you notice any patterns? Any recurring moods or images? Write about what you see.

6. Respond to the following quote by psychiatrist and author, Elisabeth Kubler-Ross: *How do geese know when to fly to the sun? Who tells them the seasons? How do we humans know when it is time to move on? As with the migrant birds, so surely with us, there is a voice within if only we would listen to it that tells us certainly when to go forth into the unknown.* Questions to consider: What seasons of your life does this bring to mind, if any? Do you agree or disagree with her? What unknown places have you ventured forth into in your life? And did these mark the beginnings of new seasons?

7. Complete the following sentence: *The next season of my life is going to be ...*

   Free write for ten minutes about your answer.

Considering "Hallmark" Holidays

Just as a puppy can be more of a challenge than a gift, so too can the holidays.

~ John Clayton

Like many of us do on such days, I called my father to wish him a Happy Father's Day. He chuckled and said, "It's nice of you to remember. Not many people celebrate Father's Day." My son also said something like that when I asked him if he and his family were planning anything special for Father's Day: "No, Father's Day is just like any other day." Taken together, their comments made me wonder, do we honor our mothers more than our fathers? Are these kinds of holidays more important to women than to men?

Americans love making up holidays. We have Mother's Day, Father's Day, Grandparent's Day, Secretary's Day, Boss's Day, Sweetest Day, and many more.

Exploring the events and influences underlying how you feel about these occasions can help you understand more about yourself. And understanding yourself helps you take control of your future.

This week's writing prompts

1. Do you tend to emphasize one over the other or make equal efforts to celebrate Mother's Day and/or Father's Day? If both parents are not living, answer this question as it was in the past.

2. Free write for ten minutes regarding your feelings about the Mother's and Father's Day holidays. Anything goes.

3. Pick one of the statements or feelings you expressed in your freewriting session and write further about it. Use this prompt: *What did I mean by .....?*

4. How do you feel about your mother compared with how you feel about your father? How do you feel about your feelings—conflicted, guilty, contented, grateful, etc.?

5. Do you think that holidays to honor certain people in our lives, such as mothers, fathers, grandparents, lovers, bosses, and secretaries are important or merely commercial "Hallmark Holidays"? Why or why not? What experiences in your life have influenced your attitudes about these holidays. Describe your most memorably negative or positive holiday of this sort.

6. What are the best ways of letting people know you appreciate them? Cards? Flowers? Actions? Other ways? Describe how you express your love and appreciation to people in your life. How do you feel you could improve or extend that expression of appreciation?

7. How do you feel about being on the receiving end of these types of holidays or, conversely, when you're not acknowledged? What do you want/expect from others? What is the most satisfying and/or memorable holiday where you were the person being honored?

THE MEANING OF MEMORIALS

Every memorial in its time has a different goal.

~ Maya Lin

In the United States, Memorial Day is a holiday that means many things to many people. It's intended to be a day to remember and honor those who lost their lives in service to our country. Over time, the meaning of the day has expanded to include remembering everyone we've lost. But it can also be just another day off work, a day in which to host family picnics and kick off the summer season with a barbecue.

Whatever the meaning of this day to you, your feelings about it are certain to be complicated. Use any or all of these journaling prompts to explore the meaning—or lack of meaning—of this day for you.

This Week's Writing Prompts

1. Free write for ten minutes about Memorial Day. What does it mean to you, and how do you feel about your response? Do you feel any judgment towards others, guilt, anger, conflict, or ambivalence? Write about it.

2. Perform a word association exercise with the word *memorial*. Do you notice any patterns or trends in the words you wrote down? Write a paragraph about what you notice.

3. Joseph Campbell wrote: *A hero is someone who has given his or her life to something bigger than oneself.* What do you think of this statement? Who have been the heroes in your life?

4. Draw a picture, or write a poem or short prose piece to honor one of your heroes who has passed on.

5. The word *memorial* is, as you might surmise, derived from the word *memory*. More precisely, it comes from the Latin *memorialis*, which means "of or belonging to memory." To you, what is "of or belonging to memory" about this day? What memories do you have about Memorial Day holidays in your past?

6. Often, when we remember something or someone who is no longer with us, we use objects as symbols. For soldiers, in general, it is often a national flag. Or a monument. For others, it may be personal objects they owned and/or loved. What symbols do you use as memorials, and in what ways do they help you hold onto memories of that person or persons?

7. Are there other days that serve as days of memorial for you? What are they, and why? What rituals do you engage in to commemorate those days?

DÍA DE LOS MUERTOS—DAY OF THE DEAD

Let children walk with Nature, let them see the beautiful blendings and communions of death and life, their joyous inseparable unity, as taught in woods and meadows, plains and mountains and streams of our blessed star, and they will learn that death is stingless indeed, and as beautiful as life.

~ John Muir

Día de los Muertos, the Day of the Dead, is celebrated over two days, November 1st and 2nd, in Mexico and other Latin countries. Here in the States, we celebrate Halloween, All Saints' Eve, on October 31st by dressing in costume and handing out candies to little ghouls who haunt our doorsteps in the early evenings. Similar celebrations occur all over the world this time of year, including Africa and Asia.

What are the meanings and origins of this holiday? For thousands of years, people of many cultures have considered the beginning of November a time when the veil between the worlds of the living and the dead is thinnest. Thus, it is the time we honor the dead by visiting their burial places, erecting altars in our homes, and offering food, flowers, toys and other items that are normally considered the province of the living.

We write poetry, don costumes—some ghoulish, some playful—and share candy and presents.

It is a time to bring our fascination and fear of death into the open, acknowledge and honor its presence as part of the cycle of life. Use the following prompts to take a closer look at your attitudes and beliefs about death.

This Week's Writing Prompts

1. Perform a word association exercise with the word *death*. Look at the list of words. Are there any connections between the words? A theme? A feeling? What can you learn about yourself from reading this list of words? Free write for a minimum of ten minutes about what you observe.

2. Use the list of words you wrote in the previous exercise to create a poem or a short piece of prose. Try to use all the words in the piece.

3. When you think of death in general terms, what is your predominate emotion? What in your life experience is associated with that emotion? Write about those experiences and what ties them together.

4. If you found out today that you had one week to live, what things undone would you finish? Who would you want to talk to? And where and with whom would you want to be in your final moments? What do your choices reveal about you at this time in your life?

5. Respond to the following question by Chuck Palahniuk (journalist and author): *If death meant just leaving the stage long enough to change costume and come back as a new character...Would you slow down? Or speed up?*

6. What do you fear most about death? What do you fear least about death?

7. Write about how the death of a loved one has affected your attitudes about death, loss, and important priorities in life. (If you haven't experienced the death of a loved one, imagine how it might affect you.)

THE "HOLIDAY SEASON"

The moment one gives close attention to any thing, even a blade of grass it becomes a mysterious, awesome, indescribably magnificent world in itself.

~ Henry Miller

In the United States, the time between Thanksgiving and the New Year is called the "Holiday Season," when thoughts turn toward family gatherings and feasts, gift giving, shopping, preparations, time off work, and religious celebrations.

Some people look forward to the Holiday Season with a sense of happy and positive anticipation. When they think of the holidays, they think of sparkling lights, family get-togethers, food-laden tables, laughter, and love.

Others dread this period as a time of stress, loneliness, and negative emotional associations. Certainly, articles on reducing holiday stress abound, as well as ways to simplify everything from decorations to the food we eat at family gatherings. A number of health studies have shown that emotional and physical effects of the holiday season accumulate over the course of our lives, so that, presumably, both positive and negative influences affect us long term—an interesting thing to consider, when reflecting upon one's own feelings about the holidays.

This Week's Writing Prompts

1. In general, on a scale of 1 to 10, where 1 represents sadness and 10 represents joy, what number would you assign to yourself during the holidays? What experiences and influences have affected your feelings and attitudes about this time of year?

2. Whether you celebrate Christmas, Hanukkah, or Kwanzaa, what are your plans this year? Are you excited or nervous? Resistant or welcoming? Who is involved and what are your feelings about those people? Explore the background behind those feelings, negative or positive.

3. What, if anything, is different for you this year than in previous years? How do you feel about this change? Was it a choice of yours, someone else's, or circumstance? Do you perceive the change as positive or negative? Write about what this change means for you long term.

4. Often, holiday gatherings are centered around food. What is your relationship to food and how does this relationship affect your feelings about the holidays?

5. Do you experience conflict between your feelings about the holidays and others' expectations? If so, describe the conflict and brainstorm a list of as many solutions as you can. Brainstorming means not judging the solutions, no matter how outrageous they seem when you think of them—just write them all down. Then, look over the list and see if any seem possible. Explore what finding a solution to this conflict would mean for you.

6. Perhaps the holidays are a bittersweet experience for you, triggering feelings of both loss and joy. If holidays bring up feelings of loss and grief, write about that grief. What or who did you lose? Are there ways you could honor that person or loss in your life during the holidays that would help soften the pain? What kinds of things comfort you in this situation? Write a conversation with yourself in which the "whole you" speaks comfort to the "hurt you."

7. Respond to the following quote by Helen Keller: *The best and most beautiful things in the world cannot be seen or even touched. They must be felt with the heart.* Do you agree or disagree? In your opinion, what are the "best and most beautiful things in the world?"

TRAVEL BLUES

People travel to faraway places to watch, in fascination, the kind of people they ignore at home.

~ Dagobert D. Runes

Many of us travel during the holidays and summers, and with travel comes planning and packing, crowded airports and security checks, delays and long waits on uncomfortable seats. To top it off, new security regulations are put in place each year; removing shoes and clothing, liquids and carryon baggage limitations, and full body scanners cause longer lines and slower progress.

Rather than get disgruntled by it all, toss aside the seriousness and use your travel time for creativity and journaling fun. Here's how.

This Week's Writing Prompts

1. While you're waiting in line or in a boarding area, eavesdrop on others' conversations. Recording conversations in public places is a good way to practice writing dialogue. Write down interesting things you hear, and include notes about accents and inflections.

2. Describe the scene using all your senses. What does it look like? Is it noisy or quiet? What are some of the background noises you hear that you might not otherwise notice? What about smells? What's the temperature like? Are you having to wait outdoors in the howling wind? (In that case, you might have to wait until you're warm enough to write). How does the seat feel?

3. Describe people that you see with as much detail as possible. Carry a pocket dictionary and thesaurus with you and use precise adjectives.

4. Once you're done describing them, make up stories about their lives. Let your imagination run wild. Think up something unusual. Why are they traveling? What do they do for a living? What do they love and hate? What motivates them in life?

5. Bring some colored pencils along and sketch scenes. Don't think you're artistic? Do it like a child, with stick figures and box buildings. Add the sun and clouds. Think fun!

6. Pretend you're writing an article for your favorite magazine. With your travels in mind, what would you write about? Traveling with children in tow? How to travel most comfortably? The science of travel? Keep communication civil when tempers flare? Make up ten article titles. Then, if you have time, write a first draft of one of those articles.

7. Respond to the following quote by Seneca: Travel and change of place impart new vigor to the mind. What do you think he meant by "vigor to the mind"? Do you agree or disagree, and why?

THE WORLD

Politics

One who is too insistent on his own views, finds few to agree with him.

~ Lao Tzu

As I write this, it is Presidents' Day here in the United States. Originally intended to honor the birthday of our first president, George Washington, it is now a holiday to honor all U.S. presidents. As is true of most holidays, many of us give little thought to its political origins and are simply happy to enjoy a three or four-day weekend when we can. *Politics* is a dirty word in some households, not to be spoken in "polite" company.

Yet, whenever I read the news, I can't help but reflect on our nation's diverse and often polarized political views, its underlying belief systems, and how we are or are not politically engaged as individuals. For instance many of us experience a pessimistic apathy about politics in general, while others of us are fervently engaged in various political activities that we hope will make a positive difference in the world, no matter which side of what fence we're on.

This week's prompts invite you to explore your own view of politics, and to take a deeper look at how you got where you are.

This Week's Writing Prompts

1. What do you think of when you hear the word *politics*, and why?

2. Free write for ten minutes about the opposite of politics. What do politics and its opposite have in common?

3. Do you consider yourself to be a politically engaged person? In what ways? What factors contribute to your level of activity?

4. When you read or watch the news, what is your general emotional response, and how do you deal with it? For example, if you feel frustrated, write about how you express or repress that frustration; if you feel hopeful, how do you express that hopefulness or not? And if you don't read or watch the news, write about why you've chosen not to do so and how you feel your choice benefits you.

5. If you could change anything at all about politics—the process of governance—what would it be, and what kinds of effects would that change make to the world?

6. Would you march in demonstrations for human and civil rights you believe are important? If so, if you thought your life could be threatened as a result (military action, etc.), would you still march? If not, how do you think you would you respond to a loss of rights that you hold dear?

7. Make a list of at least ten civil and human rights that you think are important. Looking at the list write about some of your beliefs (religious, spiritual, philosophical, socio-economic) that lie at the root of your list. Play devil's

advocate with yourself—write a conversation in which you argue with yourself about the validity of one or more of these underlying beliefs. What did you learn about yourself in this process?

War and Peace

War settles nothing.

~ Dwight D. Eisenhower

Journaling can help us reflect deeply about our personal, internal worlds. It can also help us consider broader, philosophical aspects of life and human nature.

After the death of Osama Bin Laden in 2011, I thought a lot about war and peace and the nature of hatred. This may have been, in part, because I was also in the middle of reading a provocative interview in the *Sun Magazine* with Paul Chappell, a U.S. Iraq War veteran and author of *The End of War: How Waging Peace Can Save Humanity, Our Planet and Our Future.*

In the interview, Chappell contends that what we all want, regardless of our political or religious affiliations, is to be safe and secure. We've all been taught that war keeps us safe, but war actually makes us less safe, he says, because the world is interconnected and our safety and security depends on the safety and security of all the countries around the world, not just our own. He insists that violence and war is not a basic tenant of human nature, but a learned one.

What do you think?

This is not an easy topic, but I encourage you to consider and write about it anyway: explore your beliefs and attitudes about human nature as it relates to war and peace.

This Week's Writing Prompts

1. Free write for ten minutes about human nature and violence.

2. Think about the polarization of political attitudes and the hatred spouted by media celebrities on all sides. Then read and write a response to the following words by Albert Schweitzer: *The awareness that we are all human beings together has become lost in war and politics. We have reached the point of regarding each other only as members of a people either allied with us or against us and our approach: prejudice, sympathy, or antipathy are all conditioned by that. Now we must rediscover the fact that we—all together—are human beings, and that we must strive to give to each other what moral capacity we have.*

3. When you heard about the death of Osama bin Laden, what was your response? Did you feel jubilant, relieved, conflicted, all of the above? Write about your feelings then and now, and what this man represented to you.

4. Here's another quote for your consideration—this one by Winston Churchill: *Those who can win a war well can rarely make a good peace and those who could make a good peace would never have won the war.* What do you think Churchill meant? Do you agree or disagree with him, and in what ways?

5. Do you believe sustained world peace is possible? Why or why not?

6. Write isolated words that represent your response to the state of the world today in random order all over your journal page. Use different colors if it suits you. When you're done step back and take a look at the page. Do you notice any patterns and/or predominant emotions? What are they? Select at least ten words from the page and write a paragraph or two that include those words.

7. If you were in control of the world, how would you go about ensuring world safety and security?

COPING WITH THE WORLD'S PAIN

Wherever a man turns he can find someone who needs him.

~ Albert Schweitzer

Every day, the suffering of so many is brought home to us through the TV, the Internet, and newspapers. Recent world catastrophes—earthquakes in Japan and New Zealand, tsunamis, social and political unrest in the Middle East—on top of those that are ongoing, such as Haiti, and wars, seem overwhelming at times. What do you do with all that information, especially when added to the economic suffering, political extremism, and social unrest in your own country?

Most of us, no matter our circumstances, want to help those who are less fortunate. Yet, we may feel helpless to do anything meaningful. We may not know where to focus our time and money.

Personally, I struggle knowing how to respond to the world's pain. I am neither affluent enough nor have the resources of time to help out in ways that seem meaningful to me. As a result, I experience a kind of survivor's guilt that comes from living in relative prosperity and relative safety when others are not. Sometimes, I am like a human ostrich,

142

hiding my head in the proverbial sand, unrealistically hoping the problems will simply go away. I'm sure I'm not the only one.

Through this week's prompts we will explore our responses to others' suffering and define our priorities:

This week's writing prompts

1. When you read the newspaper or watch the news and see other people suffering, how do you feel? Do you feel that you should help? Do you shut down a little? Do you vacillate between helping and hiding from bad news? Free write for ten minutes about the general topic of the world's suffering and your feelings about it.

2. Make a short list—no more than time items—of the most recent tragedies of which you're aware. Try to include a balance of international and local items. For each tragedy write a few sentences about what appeals most to your sense of empathy and/or sympathy.

3. Of all these humanitarian needs, which seem the most important, vital, or urgent to you, and why? Write about this topic, exploring what makes some kinds of suffering touch you more deeply than others. When you are ready, prioritize the above list in order of importance to you. Remember, this is about your personal, not global, priorities.

4. Make a short list of the different ways you are able, or might be able, to assist with those situations. What resources are at your disposal? Include everything you can think of, no matter how small or seemingly insignificant.

5. Free write for ten minutes about the concept of helping others. What kinds of things do you do on a regular basis

to help others? What do you feel that you "should" be doing that you're not, if anything, and how do you feel about not doing it? Are you expecting too much or too little of yourself? Write honestly, yet make a point of not "beating up on" or judging yourself if you're not doing all that you feel you could be doing.

6. Free write for ten minutes in response to the following quote by Edward Everett Hale: *I am only one, but I am one. I cannot do everything, but I can do something. And I will not let what I cannot do interfere with what I can do.*

7. What is one thing that you know you can do—no matter how small—to make a positive difference in others' lives? If that's all you are able to do, write about why it's enough. If you know you could do more, what more could you do, and how will you take that step?

CONNECTING WITH CURRENT EVENTS

Memory is deceptive because it is colored by today's events.

~ Albert Einstein

Journaling is about many things: chronicling our lives, exploring events and our responses to them, anchoring memories, emotional healing, and learning about ourselves for spiritual and mental/emotional growth. Because we are writing about are internal processes, it's easy to forget to include references to the world outside our smaller daily worlds. We might write about losing our jobs and our subsequent financial worries, but do we put this in the context of a global financial crisis and a 10% unemployment rate? Do we write about natural catastrophes in other parts of the world and include our personal responses to those events? Or do we only write about natural catastrophes that happen in our neighborhood?

Recently, while reading past journal entries, I realized that I hadn't included much about what was going on in the world around me. My journal writing practice included in-depth explorations of the physical and emotional aspects of my life, but my journals seemed to reflect a myopic view; without reference to current world events, there was no context to give perspective to my personal events, thoughts, and feelings.

To confirm—or refute—my realization, I decided to do a little research (I can do this fairly easily because I keep my journal on a computer). In my journal for 2010:

- I mentioned the economic crisis only once, though it certainly affected me both personally and professionally.

- Three entries used the word *politics*, and none used the names of political parties.

- The word *government* appeared in just one entry.

- The word *religion* appeared twice in relationship to events occurring outside my personal life.

Surprised by the scarcity of these types of entries, I wondered how I could have neglected to record the larger circumstances in which I live my life. How indeed?

If, like me, you tend to focus inward, the following prompts will help you place your life in the context of the larger world and, perhaps, give you some additional perspective.

This Week's Writing Prompts

1. Scan a newspaper or Internet news service and read one or more articles that draw your attention. In your journal, write a short, one or two-sentence summary of the event(s), and your reaction to it/them. How does it affect you to learn this information?

2. What ongoing political situation affects your daily life the most? Describe the situation and what most disturbs

and/or excites you about it. How does it touch your hopes and dreams? What does it bring to mind from your past?

3. Think about a current, disturbing world event or situation that seems large and impossible to remedy. Do you avoid reading about it or keep up with its current status? Why? What is your overall feeling about this situation? Do you have ideas that you think would help? What are they?

4. Find a piece of positive news—for example, a story about a hero or a person who is making a difference in some way. What is your reaction/response to this story?

5. Write about a world event that gives you hope for the future.

6. Write about a world event or situation that is affecting someone you know. How is it affecting him or her and what are you feelings about it?

7. Thinking about world or national events, make a list of at least five things for which you are grateful. The list can include something that is happening or an event that isn't affecting you negatively.

CONSUMERISM AND THE ECONOMY

U.S. consumers and industry dispose of enough aluminum to rebuild the commercial air fleet every three months; enough iron and steel to continuously supply all automakers; enough glass to fill New York's World Trade Center every two weeks.

~ Environmental Defense Fund advertisement,
Christian Science Monitor, 1990

In the United States, Black Friday is the day after Thanksgiving: Americans are supposed to drop everything, get up at 3:00 am, and go shopping. Similar days exist in other nations. These informal celebrations of spending bring the dual topics of consumerism and the economy to mind: both deal with prosperity, both deal with money, and both deal with closely held American values. In other words, both are rich topics to examine when wanting to understand oneself a little better.

The reason to pair consumerism and the economy is because they are often paired for us. We are led to believe that the more we spend, the more prosperous our economy will become. So, wanting and spending and the prosperity of our nation become linked. Being discontent and wanting more become patriotic. Without getting into the veracity of such statements—there are solid arguments on both sides of the issue—we can use the occasion to examine our personal value systems, exploring the belief system underlying our own feelings about consumerism and economic growth.

This Week's Writing Prompts

1. Separate your page into two columns. In one column, perform a word association exercise with the word *consume*. Then, in the other column perform a word association with the word *economy*. When you're done review the two columns. What does each column reveal to you about underlying attitudes and beliefs? Are there areas of conflict or disagreement between the two columns? Write about what you notice.

2. From the previous prompt, pick three words from each column that have the most emotional charge for you—that is, when you read them you feel a strong emotional response, either negative or positive. Write about the emotions associated with those words. Explore where the emotions come from. Are they related to things you were taught as a child? Personal experiences throughout life? Conflict between what you think you "should" do or be and who you are?

3. Would you classify yourself as a person who wants a lot of physical possessions, or a person who doesn't want very much? Explain your answer and its underlying values.

4. How do you respond to the idea that you should spend more in order to support the economy of your country? What emotions and values come into play for you? Write you responses/reactions as fully as possible.

5. Have a conversation with yourself. Using one or more words from your word association exercise (prompt number 1), write a statement. Then, respond to that statement as if in conversation with another person who has a different opinion than you do. For example, if one of my words is "lack," I might write, "Lack is an attitude, not a reality." My "antagonist" might then respond, "That's only true if you actually have a lot. Truly poor people would not agree with you at all." Continue the conversation as long as you like. Play with it. What kinds of attitudes, opinions, and internal conflicts can you uncover?

6. According to the World Bank, in 2010 the world's wealthiest 20% accounted for 76% of the world's private consumption? How do you feel about these inequities in the world, and where do you place yourself in this spectrum? Explain your responses as fully as possible.

7. What is your personal correlation between money and happiness? Do you feel happier when you are able to buy more of what you want? Or not? Think about different times in your life and different levels of happiness as you respond.

THE PLUGGED IN LIFE

Do you realize if it weren't for Edison we'd be watching TV by candlelight?

~ Al Boliska

As people have become more and more comfortable with—and dependent upon—Internet and satellite communication technology, it has also become increasingly difficult for us to unplug when we want to. With online access, email, calendars, texting, and unlimited smart-phone applications (apps), using telephones to actually talk to someone has, ironically, become one of the least used reasons for owning a phone.

Once considered the purview of teens, texting and email have become the primary means of communication for adults in their 30s and 40s. Look around sometime and notice how many people are busy texting while they're waiting in line, sitting on benches, walking, talking to others, and even driving, though everyone knows how dangerous these practices are. CNN featured a number of articles about parents who spend more time texting than time with their children, and blogger Campbell Brown reported a "National Day of Unplugging" movement, which began in March of 2010.

Books now on the market question the Internet's impact on our thinking abilities, and social scientists are taking a close look at how technology is changing the way our brains are wiring themselves, particularly in young, developing children. Perhaps more controversial is how constant connectivity has become a habit, the urge to check our email and answer texts as anxiety producing as any addiction.

The same technology that gives you the freedom to work from anywhere tethers you with invisible lines to all that you need to be freed from occasionally. Before the advent of all this connectivity, it was normal to assume that you wouldn't be able to contact a coworker or friend while she was on vacation. But now, it's expected that you'll be available 24 hours a day to respond to requests for information. Many of us even choose where we'll spend our vacation based on ease of access to the Internet.

Once in a while, it's beneficial to examine our use of and feelings about Internet connectivity—not to be critical of ourselves, but to become more aware. I, for example, live and teach and practically breathe through the Internet. Much of my business occurs via email, I use Skype to talk to my grandchildren and friends in other countries, and my passion, *Writing Through Life*, finds its place on the Internet. But at what cost, and is there a balance?

This Week's Writing Prompts

1. What is your general attitude about Internet technology? Where would you place yourself on the continuum from technology Luddite to technology junkie?

2. How much combined time each day do you spend on your phone or computer, texting, talking, using apps, checking your calendar and email? Not sure? Write down how much time you think it is, then keep track for a day or two and write down the actual time. Surprised by the result? Write about it.

3. Would you say you need to have your phone on and with you at all times? Why or why not?

4. What do you do if you need time with family or just to unwind? Do you shut off your phone and close your laptop, or do you feel that you need to always be available? Write about the pro's and con's of your lifestyle.

5. Describe a life that has a balance of technology and touch (human activities that are not technology-related). What would it look like? Are you in balance? If not, what would you need to do to move closer to that balanced place? If so, how do you maintain that balance?

6. Does your living depend on the Internet and computers? If so, write about what you do to separate work and home life. If not, write about what you would do if you worked at home to ensure that you weren't always sitting in front of a computer screen.

7. Draw a vertical line down the center of your page. Label one column "Pro's of Technology" and the other "Con's of Technology." Then write as many things you can think of in each column, as they apply to your life. When you are done with the list, write about what you notice.

INTERDEPENDENCE

Interdependence is a fact, it's not an opinion.

~ Peter Coyote

Each year, we U.S. citizens celebrate our anniversary of independence from foreign rule with parades, eating, drinking, and fireworks. We have much to celebrate: we live in a country that hasn't experienced war on its own shores since the civil war of the 1800s; we are privileged to be prosperous and safe; even in a time of economic crisis, when so many are out of work, have no health care, and worry about how we will pay the mortgage or rent, we can be reasonably sure we won't be raped by rogue soldiers or killed by car bombs on our way to the market.

Each morning in Napa, California, I wake to the sounds of birds singing, the wind chimes' gentle ringing in the breeze, and a new day filled with opportunities. But then, sipping my coffee, I read the newspaper and am confronted with the world's problems: oil spills, wars, social injustice, poverty, nuclear weapons fears, and government corruption. I read about the heroes among us who care enough about an issue to sacrifice some part of themselves to make a difference: a young woman lives in a tree for a year to prevent it from being cut down and in the process raises awareness about the dangers of deforestation; a girl raises money to save and find homes for puppies who might otherwise be destroyed; a young man befriends a community and builds a school where before there was nothing.

These heroes understand that national divisions are unimportant and that we are, in truth, interdependent. We depend on the health of people in faraway countries to mine the materials we use for our everyday living. We depend on young women in China to make our clothes and our toys. We depend on forests in equatorial regions to provide the oxygen that we breathe. And we depend on selfless volunteers to skim oil from the shores of our beaches and move turtle eggs to preserve another generation of a species.

I'm grateful that I can walk down the street without fear of being hurt. That I can enjoy the sunshine and the wine and the fireworks of Independence Day on a green lawn in the park with hundreds of other people and their families. I'm grateful that the children around me can, for the most part, live lives of innocence and wonder. And I'm grateful to remember that we are not only part of a country, but also part of a world of people, a community of communities, and that we are interdependent on one another.

This Week's Writing Prompts

1. Write about how interdependence differs from interconnectivity and how or where each affects your life.

2. Look around a room in your house and make a short list of some of the things you own that have probably been made in other countries. How do you feel about the interdependent economies, imports and exports in the world? What is the belief that underlies that feeling?

3. Select one of the items in your previous list and make up a brief story about a person who worked in the factory or field that produced that item. What is he or she like? Is he married? Have children? How is he like or unlike you? How are you dependent on one another?

4. Think about the people where you work or spend most of your day—perhaps with your family. How are you interdependent (not to be confused with codependent) on one another? Who is most dependent on you for your time, work, and input. Who are you most dependent upon?

5. Complete the following sentence as many times as possible: *I am dependent on _____ for* ...

6. Some people feel that interdependence threatens our security. Do you think this is true? Are you comfortable or uncomfortable with the notion that we are dependent on one another for our well being? Which do you think is a higher value: independence or interdependence?

7. How do you feel about the following quote by John Muir? *When we try to pick out anything by itself, we find it hitched to everything else in the Universe.* How is it true? How is it not true? How does thinking about everything as "hitched to everything else" change, or not change, your outlook?

SPIRITUALITY

METAPHORS FOR LIFE

All slang is metaphor, and all metaphor is poetry.
~ Gilbert K. Chesterton

For fun this week, we're going to play with the use of common objects as stand-ins for different aspects of our lives. This is metaphor. Then, we'll extend each metaphor as far as makes sense. If you want to be playful, you can extend it all the way to silly.

First, let's be sure we understand the difference between a metaphor and a simile. A metaphor is when we use an object to represent something else, such as, "My life *is* a river." A simile is when we draw a likeness between an object and something else: "My life is *like* a river." The thought processes are similar, but a metaphor is generally more powerful, more rooted in emotion, than a simile.

A tree, for example, is a commonly used metaphor for family. If I extend this basic metaphor (first extension), I might say, "My family is an old tree with many branches and deep roots." Taking this further (second extension), "Our branches rarely connect with one another, but the same sap runs through all of us." To extend the metaphor even further, I have to think, How else is my family a tree? Here's one way: "In the last few years, the tree has lost a number of branches, but those that are left have only gotten stronger."

The purpose of this exercise in metaphor is to help you think about your life and relationships in new ways.

This week's writing prompts

For each of the following seven objects, think about what that object represents in your life. Then use it in a metaphorical statement, as in the "My family is a tree" example. Then, play with the metaphor by extending it as many times as possible.

1. Book

2. Mountain

3. Forest

4. Air

5. House

6. Road

7. Bird (Pick a specific bird, such as crow, bluebird, robin, etc.)

After you've extended each metaphor as far as you can, free write for ten minutes about why that metaphor works for you.

DELVING DEEPER INTO UNDERSTANDING

How pathetically scanty my self-knowledge is compared with, say, my knowledge of my room. There is no such thing as observation of the inner world, as there is of the outer world.

~ Franz Kafka

Journaling helps us observe ourselves and, thus, help us to heal, to change unwanted behaviors, and to grow emotionally and spiritually. This increased understanding comes from digging beneath the surface of issues, a process that can be difficult to do with topics that are hard to write about. But, if we approach journaling with the intention of getting the most out of it, our writing has the ability to move us to greater understanding of even the most benign and ordinary kinds of events and topics.

The secret is to continue to ask and answer questions that require us to get beneath the surface. One effective method is to use the five journalistic questions they taught you in elementary school—with a twist.

This Week's Writing Prompts

Ask questions that begin with:

1. *What?*—What happened? What were the circumstances around the event or situation? What do I remember most? What do I remember least, but would like to find out? What would my husband/friend/other person think about this? What memories are associated with this event? What do I think is the truth?

2. *When?*—When did it happen (what time of day, in history, in my life)? When did I first remember it? When did I speak about it for the first time? When did my family acknowledge it? When did the subject first occur to me?

3. *Where?*—Where was I living? Where was I in my career? Where do I feel this emotion in my body? Where was my mother/father/brother/sister? Where were the people that most cared for me? Where were my friends? Where were my enemies?

4. *How?*—How did that happen? How did I respond? How did my father look? How did I feel at the time? How do I feel about it now? How might I think about it differently? How might things have been different and would I want them to be? How did my response serve me at the time? How does my current response serve or not serve me?

5. *Who?*—Who was involved? Who was nearby? Who noticed? Who didn't notice? Who did I talk to about it? Who should I have notified? Who cares most about this situation? Who cares least? Who would I have wanted to be there?

6. *Why?*—Why do I remember this? Why is this subject/event/situation important to me? Why do I want to write about it? Why do I think this story is important?

7. Finally, for deeper understanding, repeat "Why?" with the word *really* attached, as many times as it takes to get an answer that feels inspired. For example, let's say that I've asked the question, "Why do I think this story is important?" And I've answered, "Because I believe that other women could learn from my experience." I would then ask the question, "Why do I *really* think this is important?" and answer with whatever first comes to mind. I would continue digging by asking the "Why do I really ..." question until I hit bottom.

CONQUERING THE PRESENT

Presence power generates an energy field in you and around you of a high vibrational frequency. No unconsciousness, no negativity, no discord or violence can enter that field and survive, just as darkness cannot survive in the presence of light.

~ Eckhart Tolle

Have you ever noticed how children, at play, seem immersed in fascinated wonder as every moment unfolds? Have you experienced such presence in the moment yourself— perhaps when you're absorbed in a hobby or task you love, experiencing moments of supreme and intense joy (the birth of a child, the awe of a sunset), or in moments of great spiritual insight?

Most of us, at some time in our lives, have experienced an intense awareness of the present moment, our minds so occupied in the here and now, that past and future did not exist. And though we wanted to, we couldn't stay long in that present-minded state of being. Instead, our minds moved forward, planning, worrying about the future. Or backward, gnawing the bone of some past event. In journaling, in particular reflective journaling, we often spend a great deal of our energy thinking and writing about the past.

Sam Keen promotes the idea that true awareness is much more than consciously experiencing a moment in time. He said, "Awareness is only as profound as the person who is aware. We learn to see and feel profoundly as we integrate all that we have been and hope to be into the present moment. The most dynamic personalities are fully present in this moment without severing either memories of the past or visions of the future." (*Your Mythic Journey*, 1989) It was his assertion that if we learn how to be at ease in memory, the present moment, and contemplation of the future, we will be enriched and have more to give to others.

In each of these timeframes —past, future, and present— we interpret and give meaning to what we see and experience. That's just part of who we are as humans. We create meaning through the framework of images, metaphors, emotions, and the senses. Who are we, and what comprises our sense of awareness in time?

This Week's Writing Prompts

1. Describe what you think being fully aware in the present means. Do you agree or disagree with Keen, and why?

2. Describe the meaning of past, present, and future using metaphors. (For example: The past is a turtle, traveling slowly in the opposite direction; the present is a butterfly, flitting from thing to thing and never settling down; the future is the roar of a lion on a distant hill, fascinating and frightening at the same time.) You don't need to use animals or any form of parallel construction. Just write

what comes into your head. Write a story using one of your metaphors.

3. Thinking about your life so far, how do you feel about the way you've spent your time? Would you travel to the past to change anything?

4. Where were your secret places when you were a child? How are they like your secret places now? What do you imagine your secret places in the future to be like?

5. Which has more weight for you—the past, the present, or the future—and why?

6. Who were you in the past, who are you now, and who do you want to be in the future?

7. If you could exist in any moment in time, when would it be? Describe that moment with as much detail as possible—the surroundings, the culture, who is there with you, how you're feeling, what you're thinking, and what you're experiencing.

Play with these time-oriented journaling prompts. Can you make up some of your own? What can you learn about yourself (in the now) from reading your responses?

Finding the Extraordinary in the Ordinary

Within everyday ordinary people, if you look closely, you can find some extraordinary things.

~ Joseph Badaracco

Sometimes, with all the rush and hubbub and the need to achieve and learn and move forward in life, a person's eyes can be so lifted to the horizon of the future that he forgets to see the very ground beneath his feet, or the beauty in the ordinary moments and things of an ordinary day. Time seems to rush by in a blurred landscape of activity, and you become blinded to the present, not noticing the wonders that are a matter of course.

A matter of course—natural, inevitable, a river that doesn't vary its course. In spite of what we know, we unconsciously expect life's shores to be always the same. But when we discover through experience that the shape of the shore isn't certain—when flood or drought comes and the river is changed, lost, or damaged, we wish we'd spent more time enjoying the beaches.

Of course—words that take for granted, embodying an expectation that something or someone will always be there, without need for recognition. But when we cut our finger and can't use it because of the throbbing pain and inconvenience of a Band-Aid, we suddenly realize how important that small fingertip is to daily living. When, for whatever reason, people we love go away, we suddenly remember as endearing the small quirks that used to irritate us. We miss their voices, their smiles, the flowers they used to leave on our doorstep.

Life is like that. This week, take some time to find the extraordinary in the ordinary, and the unexpected in the taken-for-granted.

This Week's Writing Prompts

1. Make a list of five to ten abilities, things, or people you take for granted. For each item on your list, write what you would miss most if it were gone.

2. Think about a typical day in your life. What is one activity that you love to do and that you would not want to do without? Write a short poem or prose piece singing the praises of that activity.

3. Walk through your home and make a point of noticing everything you see, smell, hear, and feel. What do you notice that you haven't seen in a while? Write about these things. Is there any action you want to take?

4. Complete the following sentence: *The most ordinary thing about me is* _____, *and what is extraordinary about that quality is* ....

5. Pick something ordinary that you do or experience during the day and see if you can find something extraordinary about it. Write about what you find and the process you took to get there.

6. Respond to the following quote: *Do not think that love, in order to be genuine, has to be extraordinary. What we need is to love without getting tired.* (Mother Theresa)

7. Think about a time in your life when you had to overcome an obstacle or survive something significant. What extraordinary measures did you need to take to get through that time? What ordinary measures did you need to take to get through that time? Which was more critical, significant, or effective, and why?

GENEROSITY

The true meaning of life is to plant trees, under whose shade you do not expect to sit.

~Nelson Henderson

I know a generous man: he often reaches into his pocket to help someone in need, in spite of the fact that he doesn't have much money himself; he readily offers to help friends move and to watch their homes while they are on vacation; and he has been known to give of his time to help care for ill friends and relatives. I marvel when I think about him, because he does all this willingly and without complaint.

The dictionary defines generosity as "the habit of giving abundantly of one's resources to others, without expecting anything in return." The definition seems simple enough, but what does it *really* mean? The term *resources* can cover everything from money to attention, from time to affection. And generosity is not just about giving; it's about attitude as much as the giving itself—isn't it?

Like all character traits, our thoughts, attitudes, and perceptions of it are affected by life experiences. This week's prompts are designed to explore this topic on a deeper level and to reflect on the ways generosity is a part of your life.

This Week's Writing Prompts

1. Complete the following sentences using the first things that come to mind:

    I am most generous when ... because ....

    I am least generous when ... because ....

    Then write about how you felt as you wrote about times and reasons you were and were not generous.

2. Write the names of three generous people in your life. What makes them generous? Write about a time when someone's generosity had an impact on you. Was the impact positive or negative? What happened before, during, and afterwards?

3. Do you think that generosity is an important quality to have? Why or why not? Under what circumstances might generosity be considered negative?

4. Are there any famous people you think of as being generous? What qualities do they have that you admire, and what qualities do they have that you do not admire?

5. Write a word association exercise with the word *generous*. What do you notice about the list of words? What's there? What seems to be missing, if anything? Are there any memories or images that come to mind as you read the list?

6. Write about a time in your life you regretted being generous with someone. What happened to cause that

sense of regret and how did it affect you? Now, write about a time when your generosity was rewarded in some way. What was the reward? How did that positive experience with generosity affect you?

7. Respond to the following quote by Mother Teresa: *We cannot do great things on this Earth, only small things with great love.* What do you think she meant?

PERSONAL MOTIVATION

People often say that motivation doesn't last. Well, neither does bathing—that's why we recommend it daily.

~ Zig Ziglar

I don't know how to do anything halfway or how to pace myself. My bicycle ride this morning was a case in point. As I exited my driveway, I intended to take it easy and be gentle with myself; my exercise routine has been upended by work and school schedules, and I have gotten rather ... um ... soft. Last year at this time, I'd been training hard all spring and summer and regularly rode 50 miles or more several times per week. This year, I've taken my bike on the road about four or five times, total.

Almost immediately, I forgot my intentions, pedaling 18 miles at an average speed of 13.9 miles per hour. When you factor in a few hills and my lack of training, you'll understand that I was pushing pretty hard. I arrived home, huffing and puffing and sweating. And wondering why I always drive myself so hard. Why, I asked myself, do I tend to think I'm not working hard enough, even when there is so much evidence to the contrary, whether it's physical labor, causing high heart rates and sweating, or intellectual labor—books read, essays written, and projects completed?

In my experience, people tend to fall into three major categories:

- Highly Motivated individuals and perfectionists who constantly feel as though they are falling short,

- Major Procrastinators who can't seem to get up off the couch and tend to wait until the proverbial ax is about to fall in order to get motivated, and,

- Balanced Types who set realistic goals and seem to have a good grasp of what they can and cannot accomplish in any given day.

Journal writing about your level of motivation and how it manifests in your life can help you gain an honest sense of your strengths and limitations, as well as help you become more aware of how a particular quality can have both positive and negative effects.

This Week's Writing Prompts

1. On a scale of 1-10 (1 being a couch slug and 10 being a frenzied workaholic), where do you see yourself in the self-motivation spectrum? What evidence supports your view of yourself?

2. Do you like where you are on that scale? If not, what would you change and why? In what ways has your level of motivation been a hindrance and in what ways has it helped you in your life?

3. What do others say about you? Do they see you the same way you do, related to self-motivation, or differently? If you don't know, ask a few people close to you.

4. What is your emotional response to the word *goals*? Write about your response. What is its source? Think about what you were taught as a child and any experiences you might have had that would influence your attitude toward the word.

5. Respond to the following quote: *Nothing is particularly hard if you divide it into small jobs.* ~ Henry Ford.

6. How did you become the way you are—self-motivated or not? Who influenced you most in this respect? And was your response to those people in admiration of or rebellion to their lives?

7. Do a word association with the word *motivation*. Review the words you've written down. Do you see any patterns? Any attitudes? Do you see anything about yourself you didn't already know? Write about your reaction to what you see.

GRATITUDE

Gratitude is the heart's memory.

~ French Proverb

I love holidays, when families gather together and we collectively turn our thoughts towards gratitude for all that we have and are able to do and be. And so it is that when holidays occur, blogs and newspapers and podcasts are all about gratitude. To my way of thinking, this is a good thing.

It's also my personal tradition to remind everyone I know, including myself, that keeping a gratitude journal is an excellent year-round practice. The benefits of gratitude are many and well known, including:

- Gratitude takes focus away from the negative and moves it to the positive, with the result that gratitude can actually make you happier. The happier you are, the more you will attract happy people and events into your life.

- Gratitude allows you to be more aware of and receptive to abundance.

- Gratitude gives you a feeling of empowerment.

- Gratitude decreases stress, thus helping you to be emotionally and physically healthier.

- Gratitude helps you to be more generous, compassionate, and more connected to others.

This Week's Writing Prompts

1. Create two columns on a page. In the left column, write a list of ten things that are important to you. In the right column for each item, write about how you can honor and practice gratitude on a regular basis.

2. Remember an event or time in your life that was difficult for you. In what ways are you now thankful that event occurred? What did you gain from it? In what ways might you look at a current difficult event in your life differently?

3. List five ways in which your life is abundant.

4. Name one person that you love. Now write about all the reasons and ways you love that person. If you have time, continue to write about people you love.

5. Which part of your body do you like the least? List 5 reasons to be grateful for that body part.

6. Write a free-verse poem expressing gratitude for something.

7. Make a list of all the things you have that money can't buy. In what ways are you thankful for these things, and why are they important to you?

8. *Bonus prompt:* How can you develop or increase an ongoing sense of gratitude within yourself?

MOVING FORWARD

Ways to Expand Your Journaling Practice

Just as journaling takes many forms and is limited only by our creative imaginations, there are many ways to expand and enhance your journal writing practice. I have listed a few possibilities below. I encourage you to experiment and discover what works best for you.

- Set the tone by playing music while you write. Or listen to music as inspiration beforehand, then choose a quiet environment in which to write.

- Use your senses. Focus on a particular sense—touch, smell, hearing, taste, or sight—while writing. Or focus on each sense in turn.

- Journal in an unfamiliar location—at the park, in your backyard, at the library, or restaurant. Removing yourself from your usual "groove" can help you think in fresh ways.

- Write with friends. You can do this in person or online. Agree on a prompt and a time for writing. When the time is up, share your experiences with each other.

Generating Your Own Journal Writing Prompts

Congratulations, you've completed a year of writing with *Week by Week: A Year of Journaling Prompts & Meditations*! You've reaped the benefits of using prompts: they ignite your imagination, help you to think about old topics in new ways, give you the power to frame and re-frame your stories, and deepen your self-understanding and reflection.

You may be asking, "What's next? How do I continue this journal writing journey I've begun?"

My parting gift to you is to help you find and create your own journal writing prompts to provide you with years of journaling joy.

Eight Ways to Prompt Your Writing

1. Type "writing prompt" into your favorite Internet search engine. You will retrieve more links and resources than you could ever hope to exhaust. The danger with this method is that you'll spend so much time clicking on links and looking at prompts that you will not actually write! Give yourself a specific time limit—ten minutes—copy as many writing prompts as appeal to you during that time, then quit. Select a prompt, and begin writing.

2. Browse the day's headlines. Use your newspaper or browse online news resources (as before, remember to give yourself a time limit so you don't get distracted). Search any section that appeals to you: politics, local news, or entertainment. Even the comics can be a great source of writing ideas. Ideally, you'll choose a topic that makes you think and reflect about your own life.

3. Browse blogs. Another online way to spur topics is to read blogs. When a topic appeals to you, you can write about how it affects your life. For an example of this type of writing prompt, see my "BlogTalk" category on *WritingThroughLife.com*. Each week, I write about something I read on another blog. Not only is it a great way to generate writing topics, it's a good way to network and get to know other journal writers.

4. Make lists. Get in the habit of making lists of issues, problems, joys, and desires for the future. These lists are wonderful sources of writing prompts. For example, let's say your list of desires includes traveling through Europe. You can then make up several questions related to that desire, such as, "What country do I most want to visit, and why?" Not only is this exercise fun, it can help you clarify and understand your motivations and emotions.

5. Explore extremes. What are your greatest hopes and fears? When have you been most happy or sad? What are your best times of day? What's your favorite thing to do for relaxation?

6. Investigate values. Make a list of values and then ask questions about each of those values. For example, for the word *honesty*, you could ask, "Do I believe it's better to always be honest, or is it okay to tell "white lies"? Is it a lie to omit some part of the truth?" For *loyalty* you could ask, "What does loyalty mean to me? How does it change

depending on what or who I am loyal to?" Define *cheating* in a relationship. Then write about why you feel that way. And so on.

7. Explore your imagination. Think about things that might happen in a fantasy world or in science fiction. What would you love to do if you could do the impossible? How would the world be different? Would you want a superpower? If so, what would it be and why would you want it? If not, why not? Would you want to meet a magical unicorn, if such existed? What fantasies from your childhood would you bring alive?

8. Browse your photo albums. Pictures are wonderful sources for writing prompts. Choose a picture that elicits an emotional response, then free write for ten minutes about the memories, emotions, and thoughts the picture evokes.

Ways to generate writing prompts are endless. What makes journal writing prompts different from creative writing prompts, although they obviously share some overlap, is their personal nature—what the statements, questions, thoughts, or situations mean to you.

Finally, as you move on and forward, I challenge you to continually stretch yourself. Dive deeper. No matter what your answer to any question, ask: Why? and Why not? Then, ask why again. Continue to dive down through the why's and why not's until you reach clarity. Alternatively, ask how, what, when, or where, and continue to ask that one word over and over again after each answer.

Journaling is a treasure hunt, where insight and understanding are jewels just waiting to be discovered.

About The Author

Amber Lea Starfire is a teacher, freelance editor, and writer in Napa, California. Her passion is helping others tell their stories, make meaning of their lives, and access their inner wisdom and creativity through the act of writing. She earned her Masters in Education at Stanford University and has taught online, as well as at community colleges and businesses, for twenty years. She currently offers courses and workshops in journaling and creative writing. Her work has appeared in *Wisdom Has a Voice: Every Daughter's Memories of Mother,* Story Circle Network's *True Words Anthology, Enchanted Spirit, the Fiction Flyer Ezine, the Conscious Mind Journal, Inner Sanctum,* and *Voice of Adoptees.* She is a member of the California Writers Club in Santa Rosa (Redwood Writers), the Story Circle Network, and the International Association of Journal Writers (IAJW). Visit Amber's website, www.writingthroughlife.com.

Week by Week

30559721R00109

Made in the USA
Lexington, KY
08 March 2014